TOP TENS

150
FUN AND
FACT-FILLED
LISTS

Published by Collins
An imprint of HarperCollins Publishers
Westerhill Road
Bishopbriggs
Glasgow G64 2QT
www.harpercollins.co.uk

HarperCollins Publishers
1st Floor, Watermarque Building,
Ringsend Road, Dublin 4, Ireland

In association with National Geographic Partners, LLC

NATIONAL GEOGRAPHIC and the Yellow Border Design are trademarks of the National Geographic Society, used under license.

First published 2022

ISBN 978-0-00-853300-7

10 9 8 7 6 5 4 3 2 1

A catalogue record for this book is available from the British Library

Printed in Latvia

If you would like to comment on any aspect of this book, please contact us at the above address or online.
natgeokidsbooks.co.uk
collins.reference@harpercollins.co.uk

Paper from responsible sources.

Acknowledgements

Publisher: Michelle I'Anson
Head of Creative Services: Craig Balfour
Project editor: Robin Scrimgeour
Text: Richard Happer
Typesetter: QBS
Editorial: Karen Marland, Alice Grandison and Beth Ralston
Cover design: Kevin Robbins

Images
All images © Shutterstock except:
p46 (4) Xinhua/Alamy Stock Photo; p94 (1) maloff/Shutterstock; p94 (2) Jonas Tufvesson/Shutterstock; p113 (10) CC BY-SA 4.0, https://commons.wikimedia.org/wiki/File:Cristales_cueva_de_Naica.JPG; p128 (5) arindambanerjee/Shutterstock; p129 (10) Frans Delian/Shutterstock; p162 (1) saiko3p/Shutterstock; p162 (2) Vladimir Korostyshevskiy/Shutterstock; p162 (4) katatonia82/Shutterstock; p162 (5) sasimoto/Shutterstock; p162 (6) Sandra Foyt/Shutterstock; p163 (7) CJM Grafx/Shutterstock; p163 (9) EQRoy/Shutterstock; p163 (10) Veniamin Kraskov/Shutterstock; p166 (4) Richard Semik/Shutterstock; p167 (6) 365 Focus Photography/Shutterstock; p168 (1) bodrumsurf/Shutterstock; p168 (2) Paolo Bona/Shutterstock; p168 (3) diegoguiop/Shutterstock; p168 (4) Wichai Cheva Photography/Shutterstock; p168 (5) cowardlion/Shutterstock; p168 (6) Chung Min/Shutterstock; p169 (7) Skyshark Media/Shutterstock; p169 (8) lev radin/Shutterstock; p169 (9) ciapix/Shutterstock; p169 (10) ABCDstock/Shutterstock; p171 (10) Kathey Willens/AP/Shutterstock; p173 (bottom) Rokas Tenys/Shutterstock; p174 (4) PA Images/Alamy Stock Photo; p175 (7) BluIz60/Shutterstock; p176 (2) Pit Stock/Shutterstock; p177 (10) HunterKitty/Shutterstock; p178 (1) Johnnie Rik/Shutterstock; p178 (2) EvrenKalinbacak/Shutterstock; p178 (3) Max Earey/Shutterstock; p178 (4) Dong liu/Shutterstock; p179 (5) Steve Lagreca/Shutterstock; p179 (6) mi_viri/Shutterstock; p179 (7) Mike Mareen/Shutterstock; p179 (8) Bascar/Shutterstock; p179 (9) VanderWolf Images/Shutterstock; p179 (10) oksana.perkins/Shutterstock; p181 (bottom) Ruud Kaland/Shutterstock; p190 (1) Romanova Elizaveta/Shutterstock; p190 (2) Diego Grandi/Shutterstock; p191 (5) Paul McKinnon/Shutterstock; p191 (8) stoyanh/Shutterstock; p191 (10) Marques/Shutterstock; p197 (bottom) Bucchi Francesco/Shutterstock; p198 (3) Valerie2000/Shutterstock; p199 (6) Taras Vyshnya/Shutterstock; p200 (1) ComposedPix/Shutterstock; p200 (2) BearFotos/Shutterstock; p200 (4) Wang Sing/Shutterstock; p201 (8) Stock for you/Shutterstock; p201 (10) topten22photo/Shutterstock; p207 (7) PA Images/Alamy Stock Photo; p216 (4) Anton Gvozdikov/Shutterstock; p217 (8) VTT Studio/Shutterstock; p222 (1) Nick Brundle Photography/Shutterstock; p226 (5) Peter Gudella/Shutterstock; p231 (8) Belish/Shutterstock.

NATIONAL
GEOGRAPHIC
KiDS

TOP TENS

150
FUN AND
FACT-FILLED
LISTS

CONTENTS

CREATURES 8

OUR PLANET 90

SPACE 138

HUMAN WORLD 154

HISTORY 218

Creatures

Find more ANIMAL GROUP NAMES on page 39.

CUTEST CRITTERS

1

Margay

This small South American wild cat has rounded ears and the most adorable eyes!

2

Quokka

This nocturnal herbivore is known as the happiest animal in the world!

3

Bee hummingbird

Barely bigger than a bumblebee, this is the smallest bird in the world!

4 Red panda

This adorable creature is as cute as a giant panda – but is actually the size of a cat!

Their beautiful orangey fur, white throat and dark face makes them look very stylish.

5 Shrew

This tiny mammal has a big trunk-like nose!

6

Weasel

7

These small antelopes are found in rocky habitats in eastern and southern Africa.

Klipspringer

8

Meerkat

They look so intelligent and watchful as they stand upright and scan the horizon for danger.

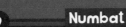

Numbat

9

Is it a squirrel? Is it a fox? Neither, it's a termite-munching marsupial!

≪≪≪ **10** Fennec fox

Its **HUGE EARS** help to keep it COOL in the DESERT and look very CUTE!

BRIGHTEST BIRDS

1 SCARLET MACAW

This large parrot with bright red, yellow and blue colours struts its stuff in the jungles of South America.

2 PEACOCK

What a show-off! The male peacock spreads his iridescent blue and green plumage to attract a mate.

3 MANDARIN DUCK

With its stripes, bars, shiny purple breast feathers and red bill, this duck is dressed to impress!

4 CANARY

Bright yellow canaries are common, but there are also red, green, bronze and mosaic-patterned canaries!

5 AUSTRALIAN KING PARROT

The males are mostly a brilliant red, the females are bright green — both are stunning!

6 ROSEATE SPOONBILL

Pink wings and legs and red eyes make this wading bird hard to miss.

7 PHEASANT

Common in the UK, the male of this wild bird has a patterned body, white collar and a head of shimmering colours.

8 VULTURINE GUINEAFOWL

Its neck and upper body have a unique pattern of black, white and electric blue stripes.

9 GOULDIAN FINCH

Red, yellow, blue, green, orange — you name a colour, this little bird is sporting it!

10 CHESTNUT-HEADED BEE-EATER

As its name suggests, this bird has a beautiful chestnut head, along with a green body.

GREATEST
APE FACTS

1 All wild gorillas live in central Africa, where the two species of gorilla are split by a vast rainforest. One side has western gorillas, while the other has eastern!

2 Gorillas are mostly herbivores. However, sometimes they eat insects and snails too. They can eat 30 kg of food a day!

3 Gorillas can weigh over 200 kg and stand as tall as an average human!

4 Gorilla noseprints are as unique as human fingerprints!

5 Gorillas are very intelligent and can make and use tools! Scientists have spotted wild gorillas using sticks to work out the depth of rivers and streams.

6 Gorillas live together in 'troops' — family groups of up to 30 gorillas.

7 A captive gorilla called Koko learned sign language! She knew over 1,000 signs and was able to understand more than 2,000 English words.

8 Sadly, gorillas are critically endangered. Their habitat is being destroyed, which leaves gorillas with fewer safe spaces to live.

9 However, conservation efforts ARE working! The population of one subspecies, the mountain gorilla, has hit a record high of 1,063.

ADULT MALES are known as 'SILVERBACKS'. These powerful males can be **TEN TIMES STRONGER** than an average human.

10

COOLEST SPIDERS

1 BLACK WIDOW SPIDER

The black widow's venom can be 15 times more toxic than a rattlesnake's.

2 TARANTULA WOLF SPIDER

During the 17th century, a bite from this spider was believed to cause 'Tarantism' — a deadly and incurable illness.

3 ZEBRA SPIDER

Zebra spiders can jump 20 times their own length, so make sure to keep your distance!

4 GIANT HUNTSMAN SPIDER

This spider has the widest leg span in the world, at over 30 cm. Bigger than a dinner plate!

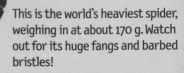

5 GOLIATH BIRDEATER TARANTULA

This is the world's heaviest spider, weighing in at about 170 g. Watch out for its huge fangs and barbed bristles!

6 BRAZILIAN WANDERING SPIDER

With a 15-cm leg span, a 5-cm body and lethal venom – this spider is fast, aggressive and not at all scared of humans!

7 SIX-EYED SAND SPIDER

This sneaky spider hides under the sand and waits for its prey. There is no antidote for the six-eyed sand spider's venom!

8 SYDNEY FUNNEL-WEB SPIDER

Aggressive and lethally venomous, the males have very strong fangs and are more likely to bite (which is uncommon among spiders).

9 MOUSE SPIDER

These spiders look like Sydney funnel-webs and can be just as toxic!

10 GOLDEN SILK ORB-WEAVER

The golden silk orb-weavers' nests hang 1–2 m above ground, so humans can easily stray into one.

SMARTEST PARTNERSHIPS

1 TARANTULAS & HUMMING FROGS

This odd couple sometimes share a burrow. The frogs get leftover food, the spiders get protection for their eggs.

2 CLOWNFISH & SEA ANEMONES

This little fish finds safety in the anemone and keeps it clean from parasites in return.

3 MEERKATS & DRONGOS

This songbird plays sentry while the meerkats hunt — then gets a share of the prey.

4 WATER BUFFALO & CATTLE EGRETS

Egrets love to eat insects. Water buffalo attract loads of flies. So egrets perch on buffalo and they help each other out!

5 PISTOL SHRIMP & GOBIES

Pistol shrimp can be dangerous, but they have poor eyesight. Gobies look out for them and get protection as payment.

6 HONEY BADGERS & HONEYGUIDES

Honeyguides can't break into beehives. They show the strong honey badger the way and then both enjoy a feast.

7 CARRION BEETLES & MITES

Carrion beetles carry mites so that when they breed, the mites will munch on larvae that could eat the eggs.

9 EGYPTIAN CROCODILES & PLOVERS

These tiny birds step inside the croc's mouth to pick food from its teeth.

10 OSTRICHES & ZEBRAS

Zebras are good at hearing and smelling predators; ostriches are better at seeing them — together they can sense more lions!

8 COYOTES & BADGERS

Coyotes can't dig very well, but badgers can — so they can find prey and root it out as a team.

FASTEST ANIMALS

NO LAND ANIMAL CAN MATCH A CHEETAH FOR SHEER RUNNING SPEED. BUT THEY CAN ONLY KEEP THIS UP FOR SHORT DISTANCES.

1	Cheetah	121 km/h
2	Pronghorn antelope	89 km/h
3	Springbok	88 km/h
4	Wildebeest	81 km/h
5	Lion	81 km/h
6	Blackbuck antelope	80 km/h
7	Thomson's gazelle	80 km/h
8	Hare	80 km/h
9	Jackrabbit	72 km/h
10	Kangaroo	71 km/h

SWIFTEST BIRDS

THE PEREGRINE FALCON IS THE FASTEST OF ALL CREATURES. IT HITS TOP SPEED AS IT DIVES TO HUNT.

#	Bird	Speed
1	Peregrine falcon	389 km/h
2	Golden eagle	320 km/h
3	White-throated needletail	169 km/h
4	Eurasian hobby	160 km/h
5	Frigatebird	153 km/h
6	Pigeon	149 km/h
7	Spur-winged goose	142 km/h
8	Red-breasted merganser	129 km/h
9	Gyrfalcon	128 km/h
10	Grey-headed albatross	127 km/h

SNEAKIEST HUNTERS

1 BLACK HERON

Black herons shape their wings like an umbrella to trick fish into thinking they're in a safe, shady spot.

2 LIVINGSTON'S CICHLID

Livingston's cichlids play dead – not to escape predators, but to kill other fish that swim by to check out the 'corpse'!

3 SKUA

Skuas fly after fellow seabirds and harass them until they vomit up their catch.

4 CUCKOO BEE

Cuckoo bees are brood parasites. They invade another species' hive, kill the queen and get the workers to raise their own young.

5 SABRE-TOOTHED BLENNY

The sabre-toothed blenny does a brilliant impersonation of a cleaner wrasse (a fish that helps larger fish by eating their parasites), then attacks!

PEARLFISH

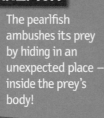

The pearlfish ambushes its prey by hiding in an unexpected place – inside the prey's body!

⑦ BUTTERFLY

Butterflies look beautiful... until they land on a turtle and steal its tears!

⑧ ALLIGATOR

Alligators put sticks in their mouths, so passing birds will think, "That looks ideal for my nest"; then... CHOMP!

⑨ WHITE-WINGED VAMPIRE BAT

The white-winged vampire bat hides in a hen's nest pretending to be one of its chicks – then feeds on the unsuspecting hen!

⑩ HUMPBACK WHALE

Humpback whales spiral upwards around a school of fish, blowing bubbles as they go – this 'bubble net' traps the fish!

COLD-BLOODED
CREATURE FACTS

1 Reptiles, arachnids, insects, amphibians and fish are all cold-blooded and rely on the outside environment to regulate their body temperature.

2 When a cold-blooded creature spends too much time in the sun, it must move into the shade to cool down. When it gets cold, it moves back into the sun.

3 Cold-blooded animals get slow and sluggish in cooler conditions. Their muscles are powered by chemical reactions that happen quickly in the heat and slowly in the cold.

4 Snakes and lizards bask at right angles to the direction of the sun to maximise the amount of sunlight they get. When the sun is very hot, they bask parallel to its rays.

5 When it's too cold to fly and work, honeybees cluster together in the hive to stay warm. They sometimes vibrate their wings to generate heat.

6 Fish that live in Arctic waters, such as cod, have 'antifreeze' proteins in their blood to stop ice crystals forming in their bodies in the very cold waters.

7 Reptiles and amphibians hide underground in winter, and their body temperature, heart rate and breathing rate all drop. This cold-blooded version of hibernation is called 'brumation'.

8 Creatures that are cold-blooded are also known as 'poikilothermic'.

9 Most cold-blooded animals live in warmer parts of the world, where it is easier to gain external heat.

600 MILLION years ago, almost all ANIMAL species were **COLD-BLOODED.**

GREAT GRASSHOPPER FACTS

1 Grasshoppers usually grow to around 5 cm but some whoppers reach 12 cm in length.

2 Females are usually larger than males.

3 A single grasshopper can eat half its body weight in plants per day.

4 In just the USA they cause about $1.5 billion in damage to grazing lands each year.

5 There are around 11,000 known species of grasshopper.

6 Grasshoppers can jump about 25 cm high and around 1 m long. If humans could jump as far as grasshoppers do, relative to size, then we could leap more than the length of a football pitch.

7 Grasshoppers have two antennae, six legs, two pairs of wings and small pinchers to tear food such as grasses, leaves and crops.

8 Locusts are a species of grasshopper. They often gather in large swarms and can destroy entire fields of crops.

9 Grasshoppers are often coloured in a way that camouflages them in their local habitat.

10 People eat grasshoppers in Africa and Central and South America. The insect is a very good source of protein.

COOLEST CAMOUFLAGE

1 LONG-EARED OWL

This elegant bird's plumage is a mottled mix of brown, black and white to help it hide in trees. It also flies silently — so prey can't see or hear it coming!

2 STICK INSECT

The camouflage of these creepy crawlies is so good that they were named after it. There are 3,000 species of stick insect and they all look exactly like... sticks!

3 SCORPIONFISH

Scorpionfish blend into the rocky seabed, which is bad news for anyone who might stand on one — the spines on their back are highly venomous.

4 NIGHTJAR

Sadly, these birds are almost too good at hiding on the ground — they sometimes nest on roads and unsuspecting drivers run them over.

5 CHAMELEON

These incredible creatures change colour to avoid predators and surprise potential prey.

6 CRAB SPIDER

These crafty spiders colour themselves the same shade as a flower, then hide among the petals and wait to pounce on a passing butterfly.

7 ARCTIC HARE

Hares are no match for wolves and foxes, but their white fur makes them very difficult to spot in the snowy Arctic tundra.

‹‹‹ 8 ARCTIC FOX

Unfortunately for the Arctic hare, the Arctic fox's white fur makes it hard for prey to see it coming!

9 GIRAFFE

You might think it's hard to disguise such a tall animal, but giraffes' markings make them very hard to spot in the dappled light under a tree.

10 LEOPARD

The spots on this big cat's body allow it to hide among the trees and sneak up on prey totally unseen.

FIERCEST PREDATORS

① ORCA

These marine mammals can weigh 6 tonnes and eat 250 kg of flesh every day, including seals, sea lions, smaller whales and dolphins, fish, sharks, squid, turtles, sea birds and sea otters.

② GREAT WHITE SHARK

These cold-eyed killers often hunt by swimming directly under a prey animal and rushing upwards to attack from below.

③ POLAR BEAR

These Arctic predators love to eat seals. Polar bears wait by holes in the ice to snatch seals coming up for air.

④ TIGER

Tigers usually hunt alone at night, stalking deer, buffalo, goats, leopards, wild pigs, crocodiles and sometimes elephants.

5 WHITE-TAILED EAGLE

The largest bird of prey in the UK will swoop low over the water and snatch fish from just below the surface in its talons.

6 SALTWATER CROCODILE

This 6-m-long crocodile lurks with only its eyes and nostrils above the water's surface and waits for prey.

7 KOMODO DRAGON

The world's largest lizard will attack animals including goats, pigs, deer, wild boar, horses and water buffalo. It can eat 80% of its body weight in one meal.

9 TASMANIAN DEVIL

This fierce marsupial is a solitary night-hunter that will happily tackle a wombat, rabbit or wallaby that dares to cross its path.

8 BURMESE PYTHON

This huge snake waits to ambush its prey, which it then quickly coils its body round and swallows whole. A python can eat prey bigger than itself, including pigs, alligators and deer.

10 LEOPARD SEAL

They might look cute, but leopard seals love to supplement their usual diet of krill with extra protein in the shape of penguins!

BRILLIANT BAT FACTS

1 A **FIFTH** of **ALL MAMMALS** on Earth are **BATS!** There are more than **1,300 BAT SPECIES**.

2 Some species **WEIGH LESS THAN A PENNY**, while others have a **WHOPPING 1.7 M WINGSPAN!**

3 Bats **SLEEP UPSIDE-DOWN** so they can **DROP STRAIGHT INTO FLIGHT** to escape predators.

4 Most bats use **ECHOLOCATION** to **'SEE'** the world around them.

5 Other than the polar regions, extreme deserts and a few isolated islands, **BATS LIVE** in **EVERY HABITAT ON EARTH**.

6 The **SCIENTIFIC NAME** for bats is **CHIROPTERA**, which means 'hand wing'.

7 Blood-drinking **VAMPIRE BATS** are **REAL!** But don't worry — they tend to prey on livestock like cattle and horses.

8 Some bats **EAT 1,200 MOSQUITOES AN HOUR** during their **NIGHTLY HUNTS**.

9 When it is flying, a bat's **HEART BEATS 1,000 TIMES A MINUTE!**

10 Bats are **POLLINATORS**, just like **BEES** and **BUTTERFLIES**. Bananas, avocados and mangos all rely on bats to pollinate them!

TREMENDOUS TEETH

1 SHARKS

Sharks constantly lose teeth — around one a week — and grow new ones.

2 RODENTS

Rodents' teeth never stop growing. Squirrels, beavers and hamsters all have to gnaw on something hard to keep their teeth at a useful length.

4 NARWHAL

The 3-m-long 'tusk' on a narwhal is actually a tooth!

3 HIPPO

The canine teeth of hippos can reach 50 cm long. They are not used for eating, but for fighting!

5 LAMPREY

These eel-like fish use their teeth to attach themselves to their prey.

6 ELEPHANT

Elephant tusks are elongated incisor teeth. African elephants have the longest tusks.

7 DOLPHIN

You can tell how old a dolphin is by its teeth — they have rings inside, just like tree trunks.

8 GOOSANDER

The goosander duck has 150 teeth that it uses to strip the flesh from small mammals and other birds.

9 SNAIL

A garden snail has 14,000 teeth! Other snail species have 20,000 — the most of any animal.

10 BLUE WHALE

Blue whales have no teeth! Instead, they have bristly filters called baleen that they use to strain krill out of the water.

REMARKABLE
RODENT FACTS

1 Hamsters, mice, rats, guinea pigs, beavers, prairie dogs and porcupines are all rodents. Rodents make up 40% of all mammal species.

2 Rabbits and hares were once classed as rodents, but now they are in a group called lagomorphs.

3 Rodents have sharp incisor teeth that they use to eat, dig and defend themselves. These teeth are constantly growing so rodents have to gnaw on something every day!

4 New Zealand has no native rodents. The only other large land mass not to have its own rodents is Antarctica!

5 The biggest rodent is the capybara, which is the size of a very large dog! They live in South America.

6 North American porcupines have 30,000 quills! And they make them stand on end to repel attackers.

7 Beavers love to build dams in streams. They will even try to build dams on top of loudspeakers that are playing the sound of running water!

8 The grasshopper mouse is carnivorous and eats insects, scorpions and snakes.

9 The dormouse is a small rodent that is rare in the UK and hard to spot — it sleeps all day and hibernates through the winter.

10 Guinea **PIGS** don't come from Guinea and they aren't related to **PIGS!** They are from the Andes mountains in **SOUTH AMERICA.**

ODDEST
HOUSE NAMES

1	Otter	Holt
2	Squirrel	Dray
3	Bear	Den
4	Beaver	Lodge
5	Fox	Earth
6	Eagle	Eyrie
7	Hare	Form
8	Mole	Fortress
9	Badger	Sett
10	Sea lion	Rookery

CRAZIEST COLLECTIVE NOUNS

1	A bike of bees
2	A glaring of cats
3	A rhumba of rattlesnakes
4	An army of caterpillars
5	A mess of iguanas
6	A shiver of sharks
7	A gang of elks
8	A horde of hamsters
9	A storytelling of rooks
10	A crash of rhinoceroses

LEADING LADYBIRD FACTS

1. There are about 5,000 different species of ladybird in the world.

2. They are also known as ladybeetles or ladybugs, and in many cultures are considered good luck.

3. They come in different colours and patterns, but the most familiar in the UK is the seven-spot ladybird, which has a shiny, red-and-black body.

4. Farmers love ladybirds because they prey on aphids and other plant-eating pests.

5. A single seven-spot ladybird can gobble more than 5,000 aphids in its lifetime!

6. A ladybird's bright colours act as an important defence mechanism, warning animals that they are unpleasant to eat.

7. These brilliant bugs have another trick to avoid danger – freeze and pretend to be dead.

8. Birds are ladybirds' main predators, but they also fall victim to frogs, wasps, spiders and dragonflies.

9. Seven-spot ladybirds are native to Europe but were introduced to North America to control aphid populations.

10. Ladybirds are happy in different habitats, including grasslands, forests, cities, suburbs and along rivers.

BIGGEST BEARS

1 KAMCHATKA BROWN BEAR

These bears can almost match a Kodiak bear for size, standing up to 3 m tall on their hind legs, and weighing 650 kg.

2 KODIAK BEAR

The largest species of brown bear only lives on the Kodiak archipelago of Alaska, USA.

3 POLAR BEAR

Standing on its hind legs, a polar bear could look in a window on the second floor of a house!

4 USSURI BROWN BEAR

This species lives in eastern Russia and its surrounding islands, the Korean Peninsula, northeast China and northern Japan.

5 GRIZZLY BEAR

Grizzly by name, grizzly by nature — this bear will easily tackle elk, deer, bison, moose and caribou.

6 EURASIAN BROWN BEAR

Although they mostly live in Russia and the Baltic countries, there are still some brown bears in Spain, Italy and France.

7 AMERICAN BLACK BEAR

They might be called black bears, but they can also be brown or even blond!

⟨⟨⟨ 8 SPECTACLED BEAR

This is the only species of short-faced bear in the world, and it lives in South America.

9 ASIATIC BLACK BEAR

Native to the Himalaya mountains, this bear has a distinctive white 'V' on its chest.

10 SLOTH BEAR

This shaggy-looking bear lives in India, Sri Lanka and Nepal. It mainly eats fruit, termites and ants.

MARVELLOUS
MARSUPIAL FACTS

1 MARSUPIALS CARRY and NURSE THEIR YOUNG in a POUCH. The word 'marsupium' is another name for a pouch.

2 AUSTRALIA has 120 SPECIES of marsupial — the most of any country.

3 Marsupials EVOLVED 100 MILLION YEARS AGO when South America, Australia and Antarctica were one big continent.

4 Today there are 90 SPECIES of marsupial in SOUTH and CENTRAL AMERICA, 2 SPECIES in NORTH AMERICA and 53 SPECIES in NEW GUINEA.

5 Marsupials RANGE IN SIZE from SHREW-LIKE CREATURES to KANGAROOS.

6 There was once a MARSUPIAL LION, Thylacoleo carnifex. It lived in Australia 46,000 YEARS AGO and had the STRONGEST BITE of any mammal ever!

7 The thylacine, or TASMANIAN TIGER, was a MARSUPIAL PREDATOR that DIED OUT IN 1930.

8 The LARGEST MARSUPIAL alive TODAY is the RED KANGAROO, which can stand 2 M TALL and WEIGH 90 KG.

9 The LARGEST MARSUPIAL EVER was a GIANT WOMBAT called Diprotodon, which lived over 44,000 YEARS AGO and was the size of a HIPPOPOTAMUS.

10 Many marsupials EVOLVED to fill roles that other mammal families play elsewhere. There are MARSUPIAL MOLES!

TOP TREE-DWELLERS

1
TREE KANGAROO

These arboreal marsupials have strong claws to help them climb and long tails for balance.

2
GENET

These creatures look like a cross between a cat and a fox, but they are actually in the viverrid family of mammals.

3 TARSIER

Tarsiers are tiny primates with huge eyes. Each eyeball is the same size as the tarsier's brain

4 SILKY ANTEATER

The smallest species of anteater lives in Mexico and South America in low-lying mangroves and mountain forests.

5 PREHENSILE-TAILED PORCUPINE

The long tail of this porcupine doesn't have any spines on it, so the animal can curl it round tree branches.

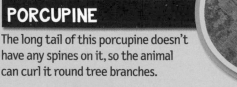

⑥ KINKAJOU

Also known as the 'honey bear' this South American mammal is a relative of the racoon.

⑦ GREEN TREE PYTHON

This bright green snake dangles in an S-shape from a branch by its tail then strikes out to capture its prey.

⑧ FRUIT BAT

Fruit bats are the largest type of bat, and are also known as 'megabats'! These flying mammals have wingspans of up to 1.7 m.

⑨ KOALA

Long forelimbs and padded paws help the koala grip branches — useful when you sleep for 20 hours a day in a eucalyptus tree!

⑩ PANGOLIN

Recognisable thanks to their all-over body armour, pangolins are the only mammal with this protective feature.

STRONGEST SURVIVORS

1

Tardigrade

Also called water bears, these microscopic animals can survive boiling water, freezing conditions and 1,000 times the radiation that a human can.

2

Honey badger

With its thick rubbery skin, savage jaws, foul odour and immunity to snake venom, the honey badger is almost impossible to defeat!

3

Diabolical ironclad beetle

This insect's exoskeleton is so strong it can withstand being stamped on, or even run over by a car!

4 ### Camel

A camel can go 15 days without water and can sweat 25% of its body's water content without becoming dehydrated.

5

Planarian flatworm

Worms have amazing powers of regeneration. The planarian flatworm can regrow its whole body from a tiny piece just 1/300 the size of its original body.

Cockroaches can shake off bug sprays, poisons and even high doses of radiation. They would probably be one of the only survivors of a nuclear apocalypse!

6

Cockroach

7

Also known as a betta, this little fish can survive in tiny puddles of water thanks to its labyrinth organ, which takes in oxygen from the air.

Siamese fighting fish

8

Camel spider

This hardy spider can sprint at 16 km/h, outrunning most predators easily. It also thrives in the harshest desert conditions.

Lungfish

9

Lungfish can burrow into mud and breathe air to survive the dry season without water.

10 Remora

The REMORA is a TINY SUCKER FISH that doesn't fear the mighty SHARK – in fact, it latches on to the larger CREATURES for food and transportation.

FUNKIEST FUR

HIGHLAND CATTLE

It can be wet and windy in Scotland but that doesn't bother these hairy beasts! They have a soft inner coat to keep in the heat, and long red outer hair to keep out the elements.

2 ANGORA RABBIT

These beautiful bunnies have super-soft, downy fur that can grow 3 cm per month.

NORWEGIAN FOREST CAT

A regal cat with two layers of fur — a warm, woolly undercoat and a glossy, water-repellent topcoat.

3 MUSKOX

These horned beasts have the longest hair of any animal — it can be 100 cm long.

5 SILKIE CHICKEN

Also known as Chinese chickens, silkies have incredibly soft and fluffy feathers.

6 AFGHAN HOUND

Elegant but tough, these dogs were bred to withstand the bitter cold of the mountains of Afghanistan.

7 SPOTTED APATELODES

These fuzzy caterpillars are completely covered in hair and have additional furry tufts behind their ears.

8 LUNA MOTH

One of the hairiest of all creatures, Luna moths have almost 10 billion hairs on their bodies.

9 KOMONDOR

Is it a dog, or is it a mop? Also known as Hungarian sheepdogs, Komondors have one of the heaviest coats in the canine world.

10 SEA OTTER

Hunting in the icy north Pacific is easy for these otters. They have the thickest fur of any animal, with around 900 million hairs on their bodies.

AMAZZZING HONEY BEE FACTS

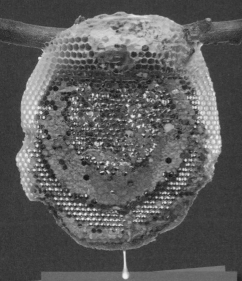

1 Honey bees are super-important pollinators for flowers, fruits and vegetables. This means that they help other plants grow!

2 Bees transfer pollen between the male and female parts, allowing plants to grow seeds and fruit.

3 Honey bees live in hives (or colonies).

4 The members of the hive are divided into three types: queens, workers and drones.

5 One queen runs the whole hive. Her job is to lay the eggs that will spawn the hive's next generation of bees.

6 Workers are all female and their roles are to forage for food, build and protect the hive, clean and circulate air by beating their wings.

7 Drones are the male bees. Their purpose is to mate with the new queen.

8 The average worker bee lives for just five to six weeks. During this time, she'll produce around a twelfth of a teaspoon of honey.

9 Queen bees can live up to five years. They are busiest in the summer, when they can lay up to 2,500 eggs a day!

10 Honey bees fly at a speed of around 25 km/h and beat their wings 200 times per second!

CREEPIEST CRAWLIES

BOTFLY LARVA

A parasite that enters its host through a mosquito bite, it burrows under the skin and feasts on human flesh!

2 EMERALD COCKROACH WASP

This wasp lays its eggs inside a cockroach, zombifying it and turning it into a living nursery!

3 WOLF SPIDER

The sprinters of the spider world — they don't spin webs, but chase and pounce on their insect prey like their wolf namesake!

4 GIANT CENTIPEDE

A 30-cm-long creepy crawly that can take down birds, frogs, mice and bats.

5 JAPANESE GIANT HORNET

As well as killing honeybees, these 4-cm-long hornets also sting humans with a neurotoxin venom.

6 BULLET ANT

The pain of a bullet ant's sting is so severe you'll feel like you've been shot!

7 ASSASSIN BUG

These killers leap on their prey's back, bite into its abdomen, inject venom, and suck out the liquefied innards!

9 GIANT PRICKLY STICK INSECT

That's not a leaf, it's a 20-cm-long insect with sharp spines on its rear legs!

8 GOLIATH BIRDEATER TARANTULA

A spider as long as your forearm! It can also hiss and shoot barbed hairs from its abdomen.

10 TARANTULA HAWK WASP

Enormous, with an agonising sting — they stalk tarantulas, flip them over and lay eggs inside them!

WEIRDEST-LOOKING CREATURES

① PROBOSCIS MONKEY

This large monkey lives on the island of Borneo and has a bulbous nose that can be over 10 cm long.

③ STAR-NOSED MOLE

This little creature has 22 fleshy appendages on its face. They help it sense prey at a superfast speed.

② MARABOU STORK

This wading bird is sometimes called the undertaker bird due to its sombre look!

⑤ HORSESHOE BAT

The horseshoe bat gets its name from the odd organ on its face, called its nose-leaf.

④ NAKED MOLE RAT

The naked mole rat is the only hairless rodent. It can live longer than any other rodent —up to 32 years!

⑥ TITICACA FROG

This amphibian lives in the high Andes and is covered with extra folds of skin. These help the frog absorb more oxygen from water.

⑦ ELEPHANT SEAL

The elephant seal is the world's largest carnivore, weighing up to four tonnes!

<<< ⑧

CHINESE GIANT SALAMANDER

This salamander is a 'living fossil'—it has existed in a similar form for 170 million years.

⑨ AYE AYE

Staring eyes, huge ears and very long fingers —this nocturnal primate looks constantly surprised!

⑩ ROTI ISLAND SNAKE-NECKED TURTLE

Is it a turtle? Is it a snake? This turtle has a neck that's too long to be withdrawn into its carapace.

WILDEST GARDEN GUESTS

1

Polecat

The polecat was once hunted as a pest, but this bandit-faced mammal is back in Britain.

2

The harvest mouse is cute, shy, and only weighs as much as a 2p piece!

Harvest mouse

4

Slow worm

It looks like a small snake, but the slow worm is a legless lizard – the only such creature native to Britain.

3

Pygmy shrew

The pygmy shrew is always hungry – it can eat 125% of its body weight in a day.

The adder is the UK's only venomous snake. It loves to bask in woodland glades.

6

When the sun goes down, watch out for brown long-eared bats hunting insects!

5

Brown long-eared bat

Adder

7

Muntjac deer were introduced from China in the early 20th century and now live across southeast England.

Muntjac deer

8

Mole

The mole lives underground eating worms, but you might see it pop up out of your lawn!

9

The brown hare has long ears and legs and can sprint at 70 km/h.

Brown hare

10 Hedgehog

The HEDGEHOG is a GARDENER'S best friend. It will happily munch unwanted SLUGS and SNAILS!

BEST BEAKS

① GROUND FINCH

The Galapagos ground finch weighs just 33 g, but it has the strongest bite of any bird.

② WOODPECKER

Woodpeckers can hammer their beaks into trees at a speed of 40 km/h!

③ BLACK SKIMMER

Black skimmers zoom low over the water, using their uniquely shaped bill to scoop up small fish.

④ LONG-BILLED CURLEW

With an impressively pointy beak, the long-billed curlew finds it easy to probe the ground for crustaceans.

⑤ AMERICAN WHITE PELICAN

The American white pelican's bill has a pouch of skin underneath that it uses to scoop up fish.

6

ROSEATE SPOONBILL

The roseate spoonbill has a long bill with a flat tip that it sweeps back and forth in shallow water in search of small fish and invertebrates.

7 **FLAMINGO**

Flamingos sweep their bills back and forth in shallow water with their heads almost upside down, filtering out their food.

8

RHINOCEROS HORNBILL

The large rhinoceros hornbill has a hollow 'casque'—a pointed protrusion—on top of its bill, which amplifies the bird's call.

10 **SWORD-BILLED HUMMINGBIRD**

The sword-billed hummingbird is the only bird with a beak longer than its body.

9 **TOUCAN**

Toucans use their large bills to pass fruit back and forth to each other.

COOL CAT
FACTS

1 Your cat's hearing is five times better than yours!

2 Cats have 18 toes — five toes on each of their front paws and four on each back paw.

3 Ever wondered why house cats sleep for around 17 hours a day? It's because their wild ancestors needed to save energy between hunts.

4 The largest breed of domestic cat is the Maine Coon cat. The longest Maine Coon is called Barivel and he is 120 cm long.

5 There are more than 500 million pet cats in the world!

6 Domestic cats share 95.6% of their genome with the tiger. The two felines split apart on the evolutionary tree about 10.8 million years ago.

7 A cat can rotate each ear 180 degrees — handy for pinpointing prey.

8 Creme Puff was the oldest cat who ever lived. This puss made it to 38 years of age — very old in cat years!

9 Cats rarely meow to each other — they mostly meow to communicate with us humans!

10

CATS can JUMP up to SIX TIMES their HEIGHT – that's like you jumping onto the roof of a TWO-STOREY HOUSE!

STAGGERING STAG BEETLE FACTS

1 The stag beetle is the UK's largest beetle, measuring up to 7.5 cm long – that's about the size of an adult's thumb!

2 These amazing insects are easy to identify, because of their red-brown bodies and massive, antler-like jaws.

3 Stag beetles have also been called billy witches, oak-oxen, thunder beetles, and horse-pinchers!

4 Stag beetles live for just four months. They emerge from their larval cocoons in late May – and by the end of August, they die.

5 Adult males use their jaws to fight rivals and impress potential mates, while females dig deep under dead wood to lay up to 21 precious eggs.

6 In folklore, stag beetles are associated with thunderstorms. In the past, British people believed these brilliant beetles could summon storms!

7 Stag beetles can fly. On warm summer evenings, adult males can be spotted flying through the balmy air in search of mates. The beetles fly upright with their wings outstretched behind them.

8 In the UK, stag beetles are suffering from habitat loss. Their larvae need dead and decaying wood to survive – but sadly, people often tidy up woodland floors and remove this precious habitat.

9 Stag beetles love log piles and old tree stumps, especially from native species like oak trees.

10 Parks, gardens, hedgerows, orchards and woodlands are all great habitats for stag beetles.

MIGHTIEST MEGA-BEASTS

1

African elephant

The world's biggest land animal can reach up to 4 m tall and can weigh as much as 8 tonnes.

2

Its name mean 'river horse', but the hippo closest living relative is actually the whale!

Hippopotamus

3

Camels are critically endangered in the wild. Their ancestors originally came from North America.

Bactrian camel

4

Muskox

This Arctic mammal is known for its shaggy coat and very strong 'musky' smell!

The world's tallest land animal has a very long neck — but it contains the same number of bones as in a human neck... seven!

5

The orca is sometimes called a 'killer whale' but it is actually the largest species of dolphin.

Orca

6

Giraffe

7

The black rhinoceros can reach 3.9 m in length and can weigh nearly 2 tonnes!

Black rhinoceros

8

Manta

The manta is the largest ray, measuring up to 7.6 m across, and has the largest brain of any fish.

9

It might not be able to fly, but the ostrich can zip along at an impressive 70 km/h!

Ostrich

10 Saltwater crocodile

The LARGEST living REPTILE can grow up to 6 m in LENGTH.

EXCELLENT
ELEPHANT FACTS

There are three different **SPECIES** of **ELEPHANT:** the **AFRICAN SAVANNAH** elephant, the **AFRICAN FOREST** elephant and the **ASIAN** elephant.

2 Elephants are the **WORLD'S LARGEST LAND ANIMAL!** Male African elephants can reach **3 M TALL** and **WEIGH 4,000–7,500 KG.**

3 Elephants are known for their large ears, ivory tusks and **LONG TRUNKS** – which are a **FUSION** of their **NOSE** and **UPPER LIP!**

4 African elephants have **LARGE EARS** shaped like the **CONTINENT OF AFRICA!** Asian elephants' ears are smaller and shaped like **INDIA.**

5 Elephant **TUSKS NEVER STOP GROWING,** so **BIG TUSKS** can be a sign of an **OLD ELEPHANT.**

6 These magnificent mammals spend between **12–18 HOURS A DAY EATING** grass, plants and fruit!

An elephant creates about **ONE TONNE OF POO PER WEEK,** which keeps the soil fertile and disperses tree seeds.

8 Elephants **CAN SWIM,** but they are the only mammal that **CANNOT JUMP!**

9 After a river or swamp bath, elephants **THROW MUD** and **SAND** over themselves to create their **OWN SUNSCREEN!**

10 These creatures have very **GOOD MEMORIES.** They can **RECOGNISE** and can keep track of as many as **30 COMPANIONS** at a time.

GREATEST GLIDERS

1 DRACO LIZARD

The little Draco lizard has a flap of skin over its ribs that unfolds into wings. When it launches, it steers with its tail and can travel 58 m in the air.

2 FLYING SQUIRREL

The flying squirrel doesn't technically fly, but it is an amazing glider thanks to the membrane of skin between its front and back legs.

3 KUHL'S PARACHUTE GECKO

Kuhl's parachute gecko has flaps on either side of its body, with webbed feet and a flat tail to help it glide over short distances.

4 FEATHER-TAILED POSSUM

Feather-tailed possums use their pointed noses and long tails as a counterbalance when gliding from tree to tree.

5 BUTTERFLY FISH

Butterfly fish have wing-shaped fins that they use to leap out of the water to escape predators.

6

PARADISE TREE SNAKE

The paradise tree snake
twists and stiffens its body
into an S-shape to glide
through the air.

7 FLYING FISH

Flying fish can hit 70 km/h as they
shoot out of the water and coast
above the waves for 200 m.

8

COLUGO >>>

The colugo is an
Asian mammal that
can glide for 200 m
between trees.

PARACHUTE FROG

Parachute frogs live high up in the rainforests of
Malaysia and Indonesia. To find a mate they use their
webbed feet to glide down to the ground.

10 JAPANESE FLYING SQUID

Japanese flying squid use
jet propulsion to shoot
themselves away from
predators, sometimes out of
the water at 11 m per second!

MOST ATHLETIC ANIMALS

1 HORNED DUNG BEETLE

The male horned dung beetle can shift 1,141 times its own weight. That's like an average person pulling six double-decker buses!

2 VULTURE

Vultures are super-strong in one important way — their digestiv system has special microbes to help them digest rotting meat!

3 SAILFISH

A sailfish lives up to its name — they can swim at 110 km/h!

4 SEA LION

Sea lions are very flexible — they can bend their neck so far back that their head almost touches their back!

5 MITE

The swiftest land animal for its size is the tiny mite — it can cover 322 body lengths a second. That's over 50 times as fast as Usain Bolt!

6 SNOW LEOPARD

The snow leopard would be well-placed in a long jump competition — its record is 15 m!

7 FROGHOPPER

The froghopper insect can jump 100 times its height in the air. That's like you leaping over St Paul's Cathedral!

9 PYTHON

Don't challenge a python to a wrestling match — its huge coils can overpower an antelope!

8 ARCHERFISH

The archerfish is a terrific sharpshooter. It can hit an insect at 2 m with a jet of water.

10 HUMAN BEING

Humans are the best long-distance runners on the planet, thanks to our ability to sweat.

DOGGY DATA

1 The pattern on a dog's nose is as unique as your fingerprint!

2 The tallest dog breed is the Irish wolfhound.

3 No wonder they have such an amazing sense of smell — a dog's nose has 300 million scent receptors while a human nose has only 5 million.

4 Dogs can't see colour very well. Their vision is limited to shades of blue and yellow.

5 Dogs dream just like humans do. Small dogs dream more than large ones!

6 While a cheetah could beat a greyhound in a short sprint, the dog would win in the long run. Greyhounds can keep going at 50 km/h speed for 10 km.

7 Dogs only sweat through their paws.

8 All puppies are deaf when they are born.

9 Yawning is contagious for dogs as well as humans!

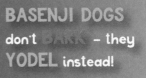

10

BASENJI DOGS don't BARK – they **YODEL** instead!

TERRIFIC TENTACLES

1 TENTACLED SNAKE

The tentacled snake is the only species of snake in the world to have tentacles on its face!

2 GIANT SQUID

This squid's tentacles can stretch for up to 12 m in length.

3 CUTTLEFISH

Cuttlefish have eight short arms and two tentacles— and colour-changing skin!

4 FLAMBOYANT CUTTLEFISH

Much smaller than other cuttlefish species, the flamboyant cuttlefish has bright pink tentacles!

5 SNAILS AND SLUGS

These garden molluscs have two pairs of tentacles. They use the upper pair for seeing and smelling, and the shorter lower pair for smelling and tasting.

6 JELLYFISH

Jellyfish tentacles are armed with tiny, stinging cells. They use these to capture prey, and sometimes give humans a painful sting!

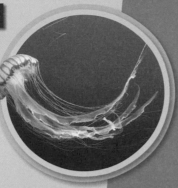

7 NAUTILUS

The nautilus is a sea creature with up to 90 tentacles that protrude from its large, round shell.

8 CORAL

The tiny polyps that build coral reefs have a circle of tentacles around their mouths.

10 STAR-NOSED MOLE

This small mammal has 22 tentacles on its face. Each has 25,000 touch receptors that give the star-nosed mole the best sense of touch of any mammal.

9 CAECILIANS

These creatures look like worms but are actually amphibians. They live underground and have two sensory tentacles on their heads.

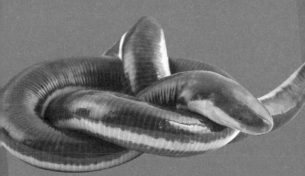

ANIMAL ARCHITECTS

1 BEAVER

These industrious rodents gnaw down huge trees to make their dams — a beaver dam in Canada was 1 km long and was spotted by satellite!

2 CATHEDRAL TERMITE

These busy insects chew up woody trees, mud and faeces — then use the material to construct skyscraper-like colonies up to 5 m high!

3 PRAIRIE DOG

These creatures design underground 'towns' with chambers at different depths to do different jobs. Nursery chambers are deep down to protect the babies.

4 BEE

The hexagonal structure of honeycomb is designed to maximise the space available for the bees to store food and their young, and to move around.

5 ANT

These incredible creatures build underground colonies by hollowing out earth with their mandibles, tiny piece by tiny piece.

6 SOCIABLE WEAVER

This bird builds elaborate nests where a whole community can live. The bird is small, but weaver nests are the largest structures built by birds.

7 BOWERBIRD

The males construct a nest and decorate it with sticks, leaves and the shiny bits of beetles' bodies to attract a mate.

9 LEAF CURLING SPIDER

This arachnid adds a leaf to its web, and lines it with silk to make a cosy sanctuary.

8 MONTEZUMA OROPENDOLA

Monkeys love to eat oropendola eggs but the birds cleverly build their nests at the far end of thin branches that can't hold a monkey's weight!

10 RUFOUS HORNERO

This South American bird shapes mud and dung into a bowl high in the trees. The sun bakes the nest hard to create a perfect refuge.

OLDEST ANIMALS

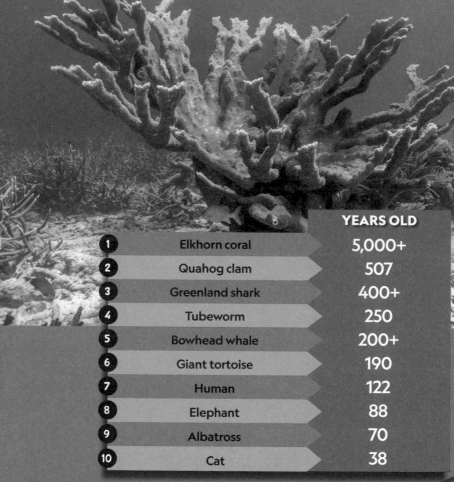

		YEARS OLD
1	Elkhorn coral	5,000+
2	Quahog clam	507
3	Greenland shark	400+
4	Tubeworm	250
5	Bowhead whale	200+
6	Giant tortoise	190
7	Human	122
8	Elephant	88
9	Albatross	70
10	Cat	38

DID YOU KNOW THERE'S A JELLYFISH THAT COULD BE IMMORTAL? WHEN TURRITOPSIS DOHRNII GETS OLDER, IT DESCENDS TO THE SEA FLOOR AND BECOMES A COLONY OF POLYPS THAT EVENTUALLY GROW INTO NEW JELLYFISH!

LONGEST MIGRATIONS

#	Animal	Distance
1	Arctic tern	35,000 km
2	Grey whale	35,000 km
3	Northern elephant seal	21,000 km
4	Whale shark	20,000 km
5	Leatherback sea turtle	16,000 km
6	Dragonfly	7,000 km
7	Semipalmated sandpiper	5,300 km
8	Caribou	5,000 km
9	Monarch butterfly	4,800 km
10	Salmon	3,800 km

DID YOU KNOW THAT ONE OF THE MOST SPECTACULAR MIGRATIONS IS MADE BY THE RED CRABS OF AUSTRALIA'S CHRISTMAS ISLAND? EVERY YEAR TENS OF MILLIONS OF THEM MOVE TO THE OCEAN TO LAY THEIR EGGS.

ENDANGERED ANIMALS

1

Javan rhinoceros

There are only around 60 of these majestic mammals alive today.

2

So rare they were once thought to be extinct, there are fewer than 400 of these ferrets left.

Black-footed ferret

4 **Scottish wildcat**

This Highland hunter is critically endangered with fewer than 400 cats left in the wild.

3

Mountain gorilla

With their habitat disappearing, gorillas are very vulnerable.

The rainforests in Borneo and Sumatra, which orangutans call home, are being cut down.

5 **Asian elephant**

Sadly, some people still kill these amazing animals for their ivory tusks.

6

Orangutan

7

The largest sea turtle species often gets caught up in fishing nets.

Leatherback sea turtle

8

Snow leopard

These beautiful, vulnerable big cats live in the high mountains of Asia.

Irrawaddy dolphin

9

These dolphins can only be found in one 200-km stretch of river, and there may only be 90 of them left.

10 Tiger >>>

There are six **SUBSPECIES** of **TIGER** and all of them are at risk from **POACHERS** and other **THREATS**.

EXTINCT ANIMALS

1 ELEPHANT BIRD

Elephant birds were 3-m-tall flightless birds that lived on Madagascar. Their eggs were the largest laid by any animal.

2 IRISH ELK

The Irish elk once roamed Europe and Asia. They had the largest antlers of any deer, spanning 3.6 m.

3 TASMANIAN TIGER

The Tasmanian tiger was a dog-like marsupial with a stripy body, like a tiger.

4 WOOLLY MAMMOTH

Woolly mammoths still roamed the Earth when the Great Pyramid of Egypt was being built — 3,700 years ago.

5 PYRENEAN IBEX

The Pyrenean ibex went extinct in the year 2000 when a tree fell on the last known animal.

6 DODO

The dodo was a 1-m-tall flightless bird that lived on the island of Mauritius, declared extinct in 1681.

7 GIANT GROUND SLOTH

Giant ground sloths were 3 m long and 1 tonne in weight. Some species were still living on Cuba 6,000 years ago.

9 COELACANTH

The coelacanth was a lobe-finned fish that went extinct around 66 million years ago — except they didn't! This 'living fossil' was found living off the coast of South Africa in 1938!

8 SABRE-TOOTHED TIGER

The sabre-toothed tiger had huge canine teeth 20 cm long, and its jaw could open over 90 degrees — twice that of a modern big cat.

10 STELLER'S SEA COW

Steller's sea cow reached 9 m in length and weighed 10 tonnes — three times the size of its modern relative, the manatee.

DINOSAUR
RECORDS

1 LONGEST

ARGENTINOSAURUS measured up to 40 M in LENGTH — longer than three buses!

2 HEAVIEST

It's **ARGENTINOSAURUS** again! This dinosaur may have weighed **100 TONNES** — heavier than 15 African elephants!

3 SMALLEST

In 2020, scientists discovered the fossil of **OCULUDENTAVIS KHAUNGRAAE**. It is thought to have been only **5–7 CM LONG**.

4 MOST INTELLIGENT

TROODON was a bird-like dinosaur about 2 M LONG. It had a large brain relative to its size, as well as stereoscopic vision and grasping hands.

5 LONGEST NAME

It's the dome-headed dinosaur called **MICROPACHYCEPHALOSAURUS,** which means 'tiny thick-headed lizard'.

6 DIMMEST

A **STEGOSAURUS** could grow to be 9 m long — but it had a **BRAIN THE SIZE OF A WALNUT!**

7 FASTEST

ORNITHOMIMID dinosaurs looked like small ostriches. They could probably run at 50–60 KM/H.

8 TALLEST

SAUROPOSEIDON had a long tail and neck and could grow to be up to **18 M TALL!**

9 OLDEST

In 2012, a species of **NYASASAURUS** was found to be **243 MILLION YEARS OLD**, around 15 million years older than the previous oldest known dinosaur.

10 FIRST NAMED

MEGALOSAURUS was given its title back in 1824 by Reverend William Buckland. Megalosaurus means 'great lizard'.

AMAZING HUMAN FACTS

1 Your **MOUTH** produces about **ONE LITRE OF SALIVA** each day!

2 Your **BRAIN** is sometimes **MORE ACTIVE** when you're **ASLEEP** than when you're awake.

3 Laid end to end, an adult's **BLOOD VESSELS** could **CIRCLE EARTH'S EQUATOR FOUR TIMES!**

4 The word 'MUSCLE' comes from a Latin term meaning '**LITTLE MOUSE**', which is what **ANCIENT ROMANS** thought flexed biceps muscles resembled.

5 The average person has **67** different species of **BACTERIA** in their **BELLY BUTTON**.

6 You **LOSE** about **4 KG** of **SKIN CELLS** every **YEAR!**

7 Information **ZOOMS** along **NERVES** at about **400 KM/H!**

8 The **HUMAN HEART** beats more than **THREE BILLION TIMES** in an average lifespan.

9 **SCIENTISTS** estimate that the human **NOSE** can recognise a **TRILLION** different **SCENTS!**

10 HUMAN TEETH are just as **STRONG** as **SHARK TEETH.**

Our Planet

DID YOU KNOW?

It takes three to five days for a Venus flytrap to digest an insect!

Find more PECKISH PLANT facts on page 102.

SUPER EARTH STATS

MASS

5,974,000,000,000,000,000,000,000 KG
Our planet has a mass of nearly 6 septillion kilograms.

2 TOTAL AREA

509,450,000 KM²

3 LAND AREA

149,450,000 KM²

4 WATER AREA

360,000,000 KM²

5 MERIDIONAL CIRCUMFERENCE

40,008 KM
This is the distance around the Earth via the poles.

6 EQUATORIAL DIAMETER

12,756 KM
This is the distance through the Earth at the equator.

POLAR DIAMETER

12,714 KM
This is the distance through the Earth between the two poles.

8 EQUATORIAL CIRCUMFERENCE

40,075 KM
Earth is slightly 'fatter' around the equator than via the poles.

9 DENSITY

5.513 G/CM³
Earth is the densest planet in the Solar System.

10 AGE

4.5 BILLION YEARS
The Earth, Sun and planets all formed around the same time from a cloud of gas and dust called the solar nebula.

LONELIEST LOCATIONS

① TRISTAN DA CUNHA

The most remote human habitation on Earth, in the south Atlantic Ocean – the nearest mainland is 2,787 km away!

② GREENLAND

The world's largest island is also the least populated place on the planet, with just 56,000 inhabitants.

③ EASTER ISLAND

This remote Pacific Island is famous for its eerie moai statues, some of which are 10 m tall.

④ DECEPTION ISLAND

From the sea, it looks like a solid island – but really it is a flooded volcano. Hence the name!

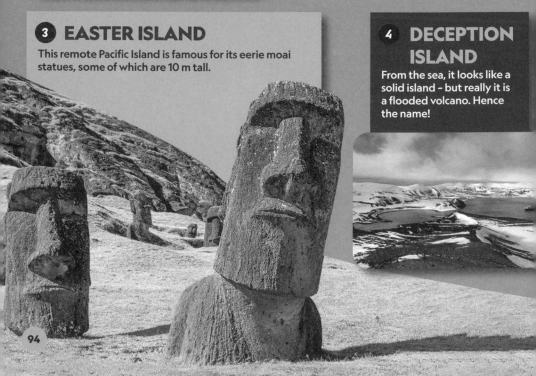

5 LONGYEARBYEN

This is the most northerly town on Earth. Inhabitants have to carry guns to protect themselves from polar bears!

6 ANTARCTICA

It's almost twice the size of Australia, but Antarctica wasn't even seen by humans until 1820!

7 SAINT HELENA

The small island of Saint Helena was where the British exiled Napoleon Bonaparte in 1815!

9 BOUVET ISLAND

Bouvet Island is almost completely covered by massive glaciers, impenetrable cliffs, and no natural harbours.

8 TÉNÉRÉ DESERT

Between Niger and Chad lies 400,000 km² of desolate sand dunes.

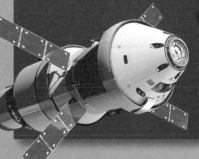

10 POINT NEMO

When satellites are no longer needed, they are 'de-orbited' to crash into the sea at Point Nemo – the furthest point in the ocean from land. Around 300 old satellites lie in this spacecraft graveyard!

VOLCANO FACTS

1 Volcanoes are named after the Roman deity **VULCAN** – the **GOD OF FIRE.**

2 Volcanoes are either **ACTIVE** (regularly smoke, steam or erupt), **DORMANT** (have not erupted for a long time, but may do again) or **EXTINCT** (are not expected to erupt in the future).

3 There are around **1,350 ACTIVE VOLCANOES** on Earth.

4 Volcanoes don't just erupt **ON LAND.** They form on the **OCEAN FLOOR** and under **ICE CAPS** too.

5 **MAGMA** and **LAVA** are different versions of the **SAME SUBSTANCE!** Magma is the hot liquid rock **INSIDE** a volcano. Once it **LEAVES,** it's known as lava.

6 The **LARGEST** active volcano on Earth is **MAUNA LOA** in **HAWAII,** which is a mighty **4,169 M TALL.**

7 Lava is **SUPER HOT** – it can reach **1,250°C!**

8 The **LOUDEST SOUND** in recorded history was made by the volcano **KRAKATOA** (pictured) when it erupted in 1883. Anyone within **16 KM** of the volcano would have instantly **GONE DEAF!**

9 Most of the world's active volcanoes are on the **RING OF FIRE** – a **40,000-KM-LONG ARC** around the **PACIFIC OCEAN.**

10 Volcanoes can be deadly, but their lava and ash help create rich and **FERTILE LAND.** That's why people throughout history have risked **FARMING** on **VOLCANIC SLOPES.**

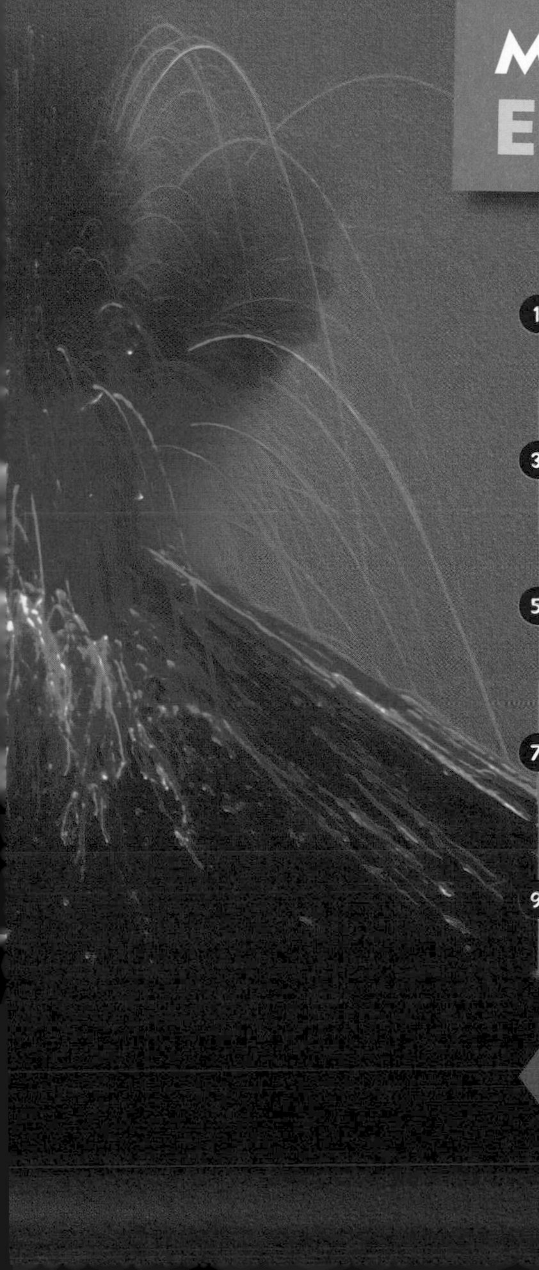

MOST EXPLOSIVE
ERUPTIONS

1 **YELLOWSTONE**
USA
640,000 years ago
8 VEI

2 **TAMBORA**
Indonesia
1815
7 VEI

3 **LAKE TAUPŌ**
New Zealand
180 AD
7 VEI

4 **HUAYNAPUTINA**
Peru
1600
6 VEI

5 **KRAKATOA**
Indonesia
1883
6 VEI

6 **SANTA MARIA**
Guatemala
1902
6 VEI

7 **NOVARUPTA**
USA
1912
6 VEI

8 **MOUNT PINATUBO**
Philippines
1991
6 VEI

9 **MOUNT VESUVIUS**
Italy
79 AD
5 VEI

10 **MOUNT ST HELENS**
USA
1980
5 VEI

Did you know that **VEI** stands for
VOLCANIC ERUPTION INDEX?

HIGHEST MOUNTAINS

ASIA >>>

All of Asia's highest
mountains are found in
the Himalayas (below)

DID YOU KNOW THAT THE
TOP 100 HIGHEST MOUNTAINS
ARE ALL LOCATED IN ASIA?

EUROPE

1	Elbrus, Russia	5,642 m
2	Dykh-Tau, Russia	5,204 m
3	Shkhara, Georgia/Russia	5,201 m
4	Kazbek, Georgia/Russia	5,047 m
5	Mont Blanc, France/Italy	4,810 m
6	Ushba, Georgia	4,690 m
7	Dufourspitze, Italy/Switzerland	4,634 m
8	Dom, Switzerland	4,545 m
9	Tebulos, Georgia/Russia	4,493 m
10	Bazarduzu, Azerbaijan/Russia	4,466 m

NORTH AMERICA

1	Denali, USA	6,190 m
2	Mount Logan, Canada	5,959 m
3	Pico de Orizaba, Mexico	5,610 m
4	Mount St Elias, Canada/USA	5,489 m
5	Popocatépetl, Mexico	5,452 m
6	Mount Foraker, USA	5,303 m
7	Mount Lucania, Canada	5,260 m
8	Iztaccíhuatl, Mexico	5,230 m
9	King Peak, Canada	5,173 m
10	Mount Bona, USA	5,044 m

1	2	3	4	5
Mount Everest, China/Nepal	K2, China/Pakistan	Kanchenjunga, India/Nepal	Lhotse, China/Nepal	Makalu, China/Nepal
8,849 m	8,611 m	8,586 m	8,516 m	8,463 m
Cho Oyu, China/Nepal	Dhaulagiri I, Nepal	Manaslu, Nepal	Nanga Parbat, Pakistan	Annapurna I, Nepal
8,201 m	8,167 m	8,163 m	8,126 m	8,091 m
6	7	8	9	10

AFRICA >>>

1	Kilimanjaro, Tanzania	5,895 m
2	Mount Kenya, Kenya	5,199 m
3	Mawenzi, Tanzania	5,148 m
4	Mount Stanley, Dem. Rep. Congo/Uganda	5,109 m
5	Mount Speke, Uganda	4,890 m
6	Mount Gessi, Dem. Rep. Congo/Uganda	4,715 m
7	Ras Dashen, Ethiopia	4,620 m
8	Mount Meru, Tanzania	4,565 m
9	Mount Karisimbi, Dem. Rep. Congo/Rwanda	4,510 m
10	Kidis Yared, Ethiopia	4,453 m

SOUTH AMERICA

Aconcagua, Argentina	6,961 m
Ojos del Salado, Argentina/Chile	6,893 m
Monte Pissis, Argentina	6,792 m
Huascarán, Peru	6,768 m
Bonete, Argentina	6,759 m
Tres Cruces, Argentina/Chile	6,748 m
Llullaillaco, Argentina/Chile	6,739 m
Mercedario, Argentina	6,720 m
Cazadero, Argentina	6,670 m
Incahuasi, Argentina/Chile	6,638 m

DID YOU KNOW THAT THE TOP 10 HIGHEST MOUNTAINS IN OCEANIA ARE ALL LOCATED ON THE ISLAND OF NEW GUINEA?

CORAL REEF
FACTS

1 CORAL REEFS are MADE BY living creatures called POLYPS.

2 POLYPS are SMALL SAC-LIKE ANIMALS just a few millimetres wide. They SECRETE CALCIUM CARBONATE to create a coral reef.

3 Most coral reefs grow in SHALLOW SEAS CLOSE TO THE EQUATOR. The reefs need SUNLIGHT and WARM TEMPERATURES all year round to survive.

4 Many ANIMALS who live on the reef CAMOUFLAGE THEMSELVES to BLEND amongst the coral.

5 The GREAT BARRIER REEF in AUSTRALIA (pictured) is the WORLD'S LARGEST CORAL REEF. It stretches for 2,300 KM and is made of over 2,900 INDIVIDUAL REEFS and 900 ISLANDS.

6 Other remarkable coral reefs include the AMAZON REEF in BRAZIL and the MIAMI TERRACE REEF in the USA.

7 HUNDREDS OF SPECIES of SEA CREATURES live around coral reefs - including giant clams, starfish, sea turtles, seahorses, eels, cuttlefish, rays and octopuses.

8 Reefs are IDEAL HABITATS for many PLANTS. SEA GRASS provides food for dugongs and turtles.

9 POLLUTION is a MAJOR THREAT to coral reefs, as is CLIMATE CHANGE, which makes the water warmer and more acidic.

10 Coral reefs are PROTECTED to help save these PRECIOUS ECOSYSTEMS. If you are ever lucky enough to GO DIVING on a reef, remember to LOOK BUT DON'T TOUCH!

PECKISH PLANTS

① MONKEY CUP

The monkey cup uses a pitfall trap to catch prey like insects and rats – using sweet nectar to lure them into a jug-like structure, before closing a lid on them!

② PITCHER PLANT

Insects are lured into the nectar-filled, trumpet-shaped leaves on this plant – before getting stuck and sliding further down into the jug-shaped trap.

③ COMMON BUTTERWORT

Lurking in bogs and fens is the butterwort – a deadly plant with sticky leaves that trap prey and slowly curl around its new meal.

④ VENUS FLYTRAP

The Venus flytrap has clam-like lobes at the end of each leaf that snap shut when an unwary insect treads on its tiny sensory hairs.

5 COBRA LILY

This plant has hooded leaves that look like a snake's head! It lures its prey using nectar, with thick downward-pointing hairs preventing any escape.

6 CORKSCREW PLANT

Like the cobra lily, the corkscrew plant also uses downward-facing hairs to force prey deeper into its trap.

7 DEWY PINE

The dewy pine attracts prey with a sweet aroma, before trapping them with its gluey leaves.

8 BLADDERWORT

These aquatic plants use small, air-filled bladders to trap small creatures such as insects, aquatic worms and water fleas.

9 ROUNDLEAF SUNDEW

The round leaves of this plant are covered with glandular hairs, each tipped with a sticky secretion that attracts and traps small insects.

10 BYBLIS

Like the sundew, byblis – also known as rainbow plants – use sticky hairs to capture insects.

BIGGEST FORESTS

1   **AMAZON RAINFOREST**
South America
5.5 million km²

2   **CONGO RAINFOREST**
Africa
2 million km²

3   **ATLANTIC FOREST**
South America
1.3 million km²

4   **NEW GUINEA RAINFOREST**
Asia
366,000 km²

5   **VALDIVIAN TEMPERATE FOREST**
South America
248,100 km²

6   **TONGASS NATIONAL FOREST**
North America
68,000 km²

7   **RAINFOREST OF XISHUANGBANNA**
Asia
19,223 km²

8   **SUNDARBANS**
Asia
10,000 km²

9   **DAINTREE FOREST**
Australia
1,200 km²

10   **KINABALU PARK**
Asia
754 km²

DID YOU KNOW THAT FORESTS COVER 31% OF THE WORLD'S LAND AREA AND ARE HOME TO 80% OF THE PLANET'S TERRESTRIAL ANIMAL AND PLANT SPECIES?

BIGGEST DESERTS

		TYPE	AREA
1	ANTARCTIC	polar ice	14.2 million km²
2	ARCTIC	polar ice	13.9 million km²
3	SAHARA	subtropical	9.2 million km²
4	GREAT AUSTRALIAN	subtropical	2.7 million km²
5	ARABIAN	subtropical	2.3 million km²
6	GOBI	cold winter	1.3 million km²
7	KALAHARI	subtropical	900,000 km²
8	PATAGONIAN	cold winter	673,000 km²
9	SYRIAN	subtropical	500,000 km²
10	GREAT BASIN	cold winter	492,000 km²

DID YOU KNOW THAT NOT ALL DESERTS ARE HOT AND SANDY? THE BIGGEST DESERTS ON EARTH (WHERE THE LEAST PRECIPITATION FALLS) ARE AT THE FROZEN POLES!

LAKE FACTS

1 **LAKE BAIKAL** is the **DEEPEST** lake in the world at **1,642 M.** It holds **ONE FIFTH** of all the **FRESH WATER ON EARTH.**

2 The **DEAD SEA** is almost **10 TIMES SALTIER** than the **OCEAN.** It is known as a **'HYPERSALINE' LAKE.**

3 The **DEAD SEA** is the **LOWEST POINT** on Earth's surface. Its shore is **434 M BELOW SEA LEVEL.**

4 **LOCH NESS** in **SCOTLAND** has the **LARGEST VOLUME** of **FRESH WATER** in Great Britain **(7,452 MILLION M³)** – more than all English and Welsh lakes put together.

5 The **5 GREAT LAKES** of **NORTH AMERICA** hold **21%** of the **WORLD'S FRESH WATER.**

6 The **LONGEST** lake in the world is **LAKE TANGANYIKA,** at **673 KM LONG.**

7 The world's **HIGHEST** lake is at an **ALTITUDE** of **6,480 M.** It lies in a **CRATER** near the summit of the world's highest **VOLCANO,** Ojos del Salado, in the **ANDES MOUNTAINS.**

8 **CANADA** has **879,800 LAKES** – more than all the other countries in the world **COMBINED!**

9 **LAKE VOSTOK** is a **HUGE** lake 250 km long by 50 km wide – and it lies **DEEP UNDER THE ICE** of **ANTARCTICA.** It is the world's **LARGEST SUBGLACIAL LAKE.**

10 The **ARAL SEA** was **ONCE** the **4TH LARGEST** lake in the world. Today after **DISASTROUS IRRIGATION** projects it has nearly **DRIED UP.**

LARGEST LAKES

1	**CASPIAN SEA** Asia **371,000 km²**	**LAKE SUPERIOR** Canada/USA **82,100 km²**	**2**
3	**LAKE VICTORIA** AFRICA **68,900 km²**	**LAKE HURON** Canada/USA **59,600 km²**	**4**
5	**LAKE MICHIGAN** USA **57,800 km²**	**LAKE TANGANYIKA** Africa **32,600 km²**	**6**
7	**GREAT BEAR LAKE** Canada **31,300 km²**	**LAKE BAIKAL** Russia **30,500 km²**	**8**
9	**LAKE NYASA** Africa **29,500 km²**	**GREAT SLAVE LAKE** Canada **28,600 km²**	**10**

Did you know that the **CASPIAN SEA** is the world's **LARGEST LAKE** by both **SURFACE AREA** and **WATER VOLUME?**

LONGEST RIVERS

The Nile (below) is the longest river in the world.

EUROPE

1	Volga	3,688 km
2	Danube	2,850 km
3	Ural	2,534 km
4	Dnieper	2,285 km
5	Kama	2,028 km
6	Don	1,931 km
7	Pechora	1,802 km
8	Oka	1,500 km
9	Belaya	1,420 km
10	Dniester	1,411 km

DID YOU KNOW THAT THE AMAZON DRAINAGE BASIN IS THE LARGEST IN THE WORLD (7.050.000 KM²)?

NORTH AMERICA

1	Mississippi-Missouri	5,969 km
2	Mackenzie-Peace-Finlay	4,241 km
3	Yukon	3,185 km
4	St Lawrence	3,058 km
5	Rio Grande	3,057 km
6	Nelson-Saskatchewan	2,570 km
7	Arkansas	2,348 km
8	Colorado	2,333 km
9	Columbia	2,250 km
10	Red	2,188 km

#	River	Length	#	River	Length
1	Nile	6,695 km	2	Congo	4,667 km
3	Niger	4,184 km	4	Zambezi	2,736 km
5	Wabe Shebelle Wenz	2,490 km	6	Ubangi	2,250 km
7	Kasai	2,153 km	8	Orange	2,092 km
9	Limpopo	1,800 km	10	Senegal	1,641 km

ASIA

1	Chang Jiang (Yangtze)	6,380 km
2	Ob'-Irtysh	5,568 km
3	Yenisey-Angara-Selenga	5,550 km
4	Huang He (Yellow River)	5,464 km
5	Mekong	4,425 km
6	Heilong Jiang	4,416 km
7	Lena-Kirenga	4,400 km
8	Indus	3,180 km
9	Syr Darya	3,078 km
10	Brahmaputra	2,840 km

SOUTH AMERICA

1	Amazon	6,516 km
2	Río de la Plata-Paraná	4,500 km
3	Purús	3,218 km
4	Madeira	3,200 km
5	São Francisco	2,900 km
6	Tocantins	2,750 km
7	Araguaia	2,627 km
8	Paraguay	2,600 km
9	Orinoco	2,500 km
10	Pilcomayo	2,490 km

DID YOU KNOW THAT THE LONGEST RIVER IN OCEANIA IS THE MURRAY-DARLING (3,672 KM) IN AUSTRALIA?

AMAZING AMAZON FACTS

1 The **AMAZON** is the **WORLD'S LARGEST TROPICAL RAINFOREST.** It covers **5.5 MILLION SQUARE KILOMETRES** and is so big that the UK and Ireland would fit into it 17 times!

2 The Amazon **SPANS SEVERAL COUNTRIES:** Brazil, Bolivia, Peru, Ecuador, Colombia, Venezuela, Guyana, Suriname and French Guiana.

3 There are **400-500 INDIGENOUS TRIBES** living in the Amazon rainforest. About 50 of these tribes have never had any contact with the outside world!

4 At the heart of the rainforest is the **AMAZON RIVER** itself, which is **6,840 KM** long and drains a network of many hundreds of waterways.

5

In 2007, **MARTIN STREL** swam the **ENTIRE LENGTH** of the **AMAZON RIVER!** Martin powered through the water for up to **10 HOURS A DAY** for **66 DAYS!**

6

TAKE CARE WHERE YOU TREAD in the Amazon – it is home to electric eels, **FLESH-EATING** piranhas, **POISON** dart frogs, jaguars and very **VENOMOUS** snakes.

7

The Amazon has the **RICHEST ECOSYSTEM ON EARTH** – 40,000 plant species, 1,300 bird species, 3,000 types of fish, 430 mammals and an incredible 2.5 million different insects.

8

The **CARNIVOROUS PIRARUCU** is one of the **WORLD'S LARGEST FRESHWATER FISH** and can grow to **3 M LONG.** It has teeth on the roof of its mouth and on its tongue!

9

The vegetation of the Amazon **TRAPS CARBON DIOXIDE** from the air and **RELEASES OXYGEN,** which is vital in helping to slow down **CLIMATE CHANGE.**

10

The rainforest **CANOPY** (the top branches and leaves of the trees) is so **DENSE** that rainwater takes around **10 MINUTES** to **REACH THE GROUND!**

COOLEST CAVES

1 Hang Sơn Đoòng, Vietnam

This cave in Quảng Bình Province has the largest cavern in the world. It is more than 9 km long, 200 m high and 150 m wide.

2 Waitomo Glowworm Caves, New Zealand

Glowworms illuminate the stalactites and stalagmites inside these caverns!

3 Eisriesenwelt Ice Cave, Austria

Near Salzburg, this is the longest ice cave in the world. It burrows for 42 km into the Hochkogel mountain.

4

These caverns in New Mexico have 119 separate caves that make a perfect home for 17 different species of bat!

Carlsbad Caverns, USA

5 Škocjan Caves, Slovenia

These caves were carved by the Reka River which flows underground through the cavern system for 34 km.

Some of the rocks have ancient graffiti on them, written by visitors who came to marvel at the cave in AD 792 – over 1,200 years ago!

6

Reed Flute Cave, Chi

7

Luray Caverns, USA

Here you'll find a unique musical instrument. The Great Stalacpipe Organ uses mallets to hit stalactites of different sizes to produce notes!

8

Mulu Caves, Borneo

Among these caves is one of the largest caverns in the world, with waterfalls up to 122 m high.

9

Mammoth Cave, USA

Kentucky has one of the longest cave systems in the world, with over 650 km of subterranean passageways – further than the distance from London to Edinburgh!

10

Cave of Crystals, Mexico

Home to some of the **LARGEST** natural **CRYSTALS** ever found. These spears of GYPSUM can reach 11 m long and weigh 12 tonnes. »

EARTHQUAKE FACTS

1 The Earth's crust is not one solid piece. It is more like a 20-piece jigsaw. The pieces are called 'plates'.

2 Plates in the Earth's crust move very slowly against each other. When they rub or split apart, earthquakes can happen.

3 Most earthquakes are so tiny, or happen so deep inside the Earth, that we don't feel them.

4 Around half a million quakes shake the Earth every day!

5 Sometimes earthquakes are big enough to cause serious damage and can be felt thousands of kilometres away.

6 Japan records more earthquakes than any other country.

7 Earthquakes can cause tsunamis, landslides, flooding and building collapses.

8 The most powerful earthquake ever recorded happened in 1960 in Valdivia in Chile, with a magnitude of 9.5. It lasted for ten minutes.

9 The Valdivia earthquake created a tsunami that travelled 10,000 km across the Pacific Ocean to Hawaii.

10 Earthquakes can happen slowly—a quake in 1861 in Sumatra marked the end of a rumble in the Earth that had lasted 32 years!

DEADLIEST
EARTHQUAKES

		YEAR	MAGNITUDE	DEATHS
1	Shaanxi, China	1556	8	830,000
2	Port-au-Prince, Haiti	2010	7	316,000
3	Haiyuan, China	1920	8.25	273,000
4	Antioch, Turkey	115	7.5	260,000
5	Antioch, Turkey	526	7	250,000
6	Tangshan, China	1976	7.6	243,000
7	Sumatra, Indonesia	2004	9.1	230,000
8	Ganja, Azerbaijan	1139	7.7	230,000
9	Damghan, Iran	856	7.9	200,000
10	Dvin, Armenia	893	8.3	150,000

LARGEST OCEANS & SEAS

1 PACIFIC OCEAN
168.7 million km²

2 ATLANTIC OCEAN
85.1 million km²

3 INDIAN OCEAN
70.6 million km²

4 SOUTHERN OCEAN
22 million km²

5 ARCTIC OCEAN
15.6 million km²

6 PHILIPPINE SEA
5.7 million km²

7 CORAL SEA
4.8 million km²

8 ARABIAN SEA
3.9 million km²

9 SOUTH CHINA SEA
3.5 million km²

10 CARIBBEAN SEA
2.7 million km²

DID YOU KNOW THAT THE WORLD'S OCEANS AND SEAS COVER 70.8% OF THE EARTH'S SURFACE AND CONTAIN 97% OF EARTH'S WATER?

DEEPEST OCEANIC TRENCHES

	DEEPEST POINT	LOCATION	DEPTH
1 MARIANA TRENCH	Challenger Deep	Pacific Ocean	10,924 m
2 TONGA TRENCH	Horizon Deep	Pacific Ocean	10,816 m
3 PHILIPPINE TRENCH	Emden Deep	Pacific Ocean	10,540 m
4 KURIL TRENCH	unnamed	Pacific Ocean	10,540 m
5 KERMADEC TRENCH	unnamed	Pacific Ocean	10,047 m
6 IZU-OGASAWARA TRENCH	unnamed	Pacific Ocean	9,810 m
7 NEW BRITAIN TRENCH	Planet Deep	Solomon Sea	9,140 m
8 JAPAN TRENCH	unnamed	Pacific Ocean	8,412 m
9 PUERTO RICO TRENCH	Milwaukee Deep	Caribbean Sea	8,378 m
10 SOUTH SANDWICH TRENCH	Meteor Depth	Atlantic Ocean	8,265 m

DID YOU KNOW THAT THE WORLD RECORD FOR THE FIRST SOLO DESCENT INTO THE CHALLENGER DEEP WAS ACHIEVED IN 2012 BY FILM DIRECTOR JAMES CAMERON? HE PILOTED THE DEEPSEA CHALLENGER VESSEL TO A DEPTH OF 10.908 M.

ISLAND FACTS

1. An **ARCHIPELAGO** is a **GROUP OF ISLANDS**. The **MALAY ARCHIPELAGO** is the **LARGEST** in the world, with more than **25,000** separate islands.

2. About **1 IN 6 PEOPLE** on Earth **LIVE ON AN ISLAND.**

3. The **GALÁPAGOS ISLANDS** are so rich in amazing animals and natural beauty that **97%** of the area is a **PROTECTED NATIONAL PARK.**

4. **PIG BEACH ISLAND** in the **BAHAMAS** is unique – it is inhabited only by **SWIMMING PIGS!**

5. All Olympic **CURLING STONES** are made from **GRANITE** quarried from **AILSA CRAIG**, a tiny **SCOTTISH ISLAND.**

6. The **SENTINELESE** are an **INDIGENOUS TRIBE** of people who live on **NORTH SENTINEL ISLAND**, completely **CUT OFF** from the rest of **HUMANITY.**

7. The **MOST POPULOUS** island is **JAVA** with over **130 MILLION PEOPLE.**

8. Don't set foot on **ILHA DA QUEIMADA GRANDE** – this Brazilian island is completely **OVERRUN WITH POISONOUS SNAKES!**

9. **VULCAN POINT** is an **ISLAND** in a **LAKE** on an **ISLAND** in a **LAKE** on an **ISLAND!** This rocky outcrop lies in Main Crater Lake on Taal Volcano in Taal Lake on Luzon Island in the **PHILIPPINES.**

10. Sometimes clumps of **PLANTS, BRANCHES** and **SOIL** are torn away from land to become **SMALL, FLOATING ISLANDS.**

LARGEST ISLANDS

1	**GREENLAND** 2,130,800 km²	**NEW GUINEA** 785,753 km² **2**
3	**BORNEO** 748,168 km²	**MADAGASCAR** 587,041 km² **4**
5	**BAFFIN ISLAND** 507,451 km²	**SUMATRA** 443,065 km² **6**
7	**HONSHU** 225,800 km²	**VICTORIA ISLAND** 217,291 km² **8**
9	**GREAT BRITAIN** 209,331 km²	**ELLESMERE ISLAND** 196,236 km² **10**

Did you know that **AUSTRALIA** would be the biggest island, but it is **CLASSED AS A CONTINENT?**

FANTASTIC POLAR FACTS

2 When it's **SUMMER** in the Arctic, it is **WINTER** in the Antarctic – and **VICE VERSA.**

1 The **ARCTIC** is the cold and icy region around Earth's **NORTH POLE.** The **ANTARCTIC** surrounds the **SOUTH POLE.**

3 **UNDER** the ice of the **ANTARCTIC** lies the continent of **ANTARCTICA,** 98% of which is covered in **ICE.** This ice sheet is 2.1 km thick on average – and 4.8 km thick in some places!

4 Because **POLAR BEARS** live in the **ARCTIC** and **PENGUINS** live in the **ANTARCTIC,** they could never meet in the wild!

5 The Arctic and Antarctic are **POLAR DESERTS.** The South Pole gets **LESS THAN 50 MM** of **PRECIPITATION** (in the form of snow) per **YEAR.**

6 In 1978, **EMILIO MARCOS PALMA** did something no human had ever done before – he was **BORN IN THE ANTARCTIC!**

7 **ARCTIC ICE** holds **10%** of the **WORLD'S FRESH WATER.** The ice is very important to the Earth's climate.

8 **2 MILLION PEOPLE** live in the **ARCTIC.** Indigenous groups, such as the **INUIT,** have adapted to live in harsh conditions.

9 The **ANTARCTIC** contains **70%** of the **WORLD'S FRESH WATER** and **90%** of its **ICE.**

10 **ANTARCTICA** is the **HIGHEST, DRIEST, COLDEST** and **WINDIEST** continent on Earth.

INCREDIBLE ICE AGE INFO

1 When the climate is very cold for a long time, huge ice sheets can cover the land. This is known as an ice age.

2 There have been at least five major ice ages. The last ice age ended 11,700 years ago.

3 In the last ice age one third of the planet was covered in ice.

4 With so much water locked up in ice sheets, the sea level was 100 m lower than it is today.

5 In a severe ice age, glacial ice sheets can reach the equator. This is called a 'snowball Earth'.

6 Ice ages are caused by factors including changes in the Earth's position relative to the sun, the planet's tilt, the atmosphere and ocean currents.

7 As glaciers grow during ice ages, they carve out valleys and move rocks around.

8 Our human ancestors probably lived in caves during the last ice age.

9 There were no modern weapons or tools. Killing a cave bear, mammoth or sabre-tooth cat with only a spear would have been quite a challenge!

10 During the last ice age there were glyptodons – armadillos the size of small cars – and giant beavers the size of bears!

GOBSMACKING GLACIER FACTS

1 Glaciers are like huge rivers of ice that 'flow' very slowly from snowy mountains towards the sea. They form over hundreds of years where fallen snow compresses and turns into ice.

2 10% of Earth's land is covered with glacial ice. During the last ice age glaciers covered 32% of the land.

3 Glacial ice is so dense and compact that it is often a vibrant shade of blue!

4 There are two main types of glaciers: Alpine glaciers, which form on mountainsides, and Continental ice sheets, which spread out and cover larger areas.

5 Glaciers are the world's biggest reserve of fresh water – 75%, in fact!

6 The world's largest glacier is Lambert Glacier, in Antarctica. It is a mighty 100 km wide, 400 km long and 2.5 km deep.

7 The Kutiah Glacier in Pakistan has the record for the fastest glacier surge. In 1953, it moved more than 12 km in three months.

8 Glacial ice can be hundreds of thousands of years old, making it ideal for measuring climate change.

9 Earth's two ice sheets cover most of Greenland and Antarctica and make up more than 99% of the world's glacial ice.

10 If the Antarctic ice sheet melted completely, sea levels would rise by around 65 m. London and New York are just two of the many cities that would be lost under water!

FANTASTIC
FOSSIL FINDS

1 LUCY is a 3.2-million-year-old FOSSIL of an AUSTRALOPITHECUS – an ANCESTOR of modern HUMANS. She was found in Ethiopia in 1974.

2 When the FEMUR of a MEGALOSAURUS was dug up in England in 1676, it was thought to be the LEG BONE of a human GIANT!

3 The SKELETON of MOSASAURUS found in 1764 was the first fossil that scientists realised came from an EXTINCT SPECIES.

4 The first FULL DINOSAUR fossil ever EXCAVATED in the USA was HADROSAURUS in 1858.

5 The discovery of ARCHAEOPTERYX in 1862 provided the perfect 'MISSING LINK' between DINOSAURS and BIRDS.

6 The BEST-PRESERVED dinosaur fossil is a near-perfect specimen of BOREALOPELTA MARKMITCHELLI, an armoured creature that lived about 110 MILLION YEARS AGO.

7 The LARGEST and most complete T-REX fossil is called SUE after its finder, palaeontologist Susan Hendrickson, who discovered the remains in South Dakota in 1990.

8 Fossils of ARGENTINOSAURUS suggest it was the LARGEST land creature OF ALL TIME. It was 40 M LONG and weighed up to 100 TONNES!

9 YUTYRANNUS, discovered in 2012, was a TYRANNOSAUR fossil that had a coat of FEATHERS!

10 The world's OLDEST fossils are STROMATOLITES, colonies of ANCIENT BACTERIA, found in 3.7-billion-year-old rocks in Greenland.

TALLEST WATERFALLS

1

ANGEL FALLS
Venezuela
979 m

2

TUGELA
South Africa
948 m

3

UTGÅRD
Norway
800 m

4

MONGEFOSSEN
Norway
774 m

5

MTARAZI
Zimbabwe
762 m

6

YOSEMITE
USA
739 m

7

MARDALSFOSSEN
Norway
657 m

8

TYSSESTRENGENE
Norway
646 m

9

CUQUENAN
Venezuela
610 m

10

SUTHERLAND
New Zealand
580m

DID YOU KNOW THAT ANGEL FALLS AND THE SURROUNDING CANAIMA NATIONAL PARK IN VENEZUELA WERE THE INSPIRATION FOR PARADISE FALLS IN THE DISNEY/PIXAR MOVIE 'UP'?

DEEPEST CANYONS

		LOCATION	DEPTH
1	YARLUNG ZANGBO CANYON	China	5,382 m
2	KALI GANDAKI CANYON	Nepal	4,403 m
3	TIGER LEAPING GORGE	China	3,790 m
4	COTAHUASI CANYON	Peru	3,535 m
5	COLCA CANYON	Peru	3,200 m
6	HELLS CANYON	USA	2,412 m
7	URIQUE CANYON	Mexico	1,879 m
8	GRAND CANYON	USA	1,829 m
9	BLYDE RIVER CANYON	South Africa	1,383 m
10	TARA RIVER CANYON	Montenegro	1,300 m

DID YOU KNOW THAT, AS WELL AS BEING THE DEEPEST CANYON IN THE WORLD, THE YARLUNG ZANGBO CANYON IS ALSO ONE OF THE LONGEST? IT STRETCHES FOR MORE THAN 500 KM!

DEADLIEST DISASTERS

1 YANGTZE RIVER FLOOD, 1931

The deadliest natural disaster in history flooded an area larger than England and **4 MILLION** people lost their lives.

2 YELLOW RIVER FLOOD, 1887

The rain-swollen river burst through dikes and flooded a huge area of farmland, sweeping away nearly **1 MILLION** people.

3 SHAANXI EARTHQUAKE, 1556

The deadliest earthquake in history devastated China's Shaanxi province and **830,000** people perished.

4 BHOLA CYCLONE, 1970

Winds of 200 km/h and a 10.6-m storm surge wreaked havoc in the low-lying islands of the Bay of Bengal. There were as many as **500,000** deaths.

5 HAITI EARTHQUAKE, 2010

Over 3 million people in this country were affected by the quake and **316,000** lost their lives.

6 CORINGA CYCLONE, 1839

The whirling winds of this cyclone created a 12-m-high storm surge, killing **300,000** people.

7 HAIYUAN EARTHQUAKE, 1920

The quake that rocked north central China's Haiyuan County triggered deadly landslides and over **273,000** lives were lost.

8 ANTIOCH EARTHQUAKES, AD 115 AND AD 526

At least **250,000** people perished in each of these two quakes in ancient Syria.

9 TANGSHAN EARTHQUAKE, 1976

The Chinese city of Tangshan was completely flattened by a magnitude 7.6 earthquake with **243,000** deaths.

10 INDIAN OCEAN TSUNAMI, 2004

When a 9.1 magnitude earthquake struck undersea off Sumatra, Indonesia, it caused a 30-m-high tsunami that killed **230,000** people.

WEIRDEST WEATHER

1. Around 1,800 thunderstorms are shaking the skies at this very moment around the world. That's a total of 16 million a year!

2. The average thunderstorm is 24 km in diameter and lasts around 30 minutes.

3. 'Blood rain' fell in Kerala, India, in July 2001. It wasn't actually blood, but red algae spores in the water droplets.

4. It can rain animals! Small creatures such as frogs, lizards and fish can get swept up in waterspouts and then fall to Earth with raindrops.

5. When dirt gets whipped up by strong winds it can create dust storms called black blizzards.

6. 'Sundogs' look like a halo around the sun. They form when the sun is low and its rays are deflected by tiny ice crystals in the clouds.

7. 'Fogbows' are white rainbows. They happen when sunlight is reflected from the water droplets in dense fog.

8. When a wildfire gets big it can create its own wind and give birth to tornadoes made of fire called fire whirls, or fire devils.

9. Noctilucent clouds are the highest in the world, stretching more than 80 km up to the edge of space.

10. Morning glory clouds look like huge tubes rolling across the sky, stretching up to 1,000 km long.

WILDEST
WEATHER RECORDS

COLDEST	-89.2°C on 21 July 1983 in Vostok Station, Antarctica
HOTTEST	56.7°C on 10 July 1913 in Furnace Creek, California, USA
DRIEST	Less than 0.2 mm of rain per year at Quillagua, Chile
WETTEST	12.7 m of rain per year at Mawsynram, India
FASTEST WIND	484 km/h in a tornado on 3 May 1999 in Oklahoma, USA
HEAVIEST SNOWFALL	256 cm on 5 March 2015 in Capracotta, Italy
SUNNIEST	4,015 hours per year in Yuma, Arizona, USA
BIGGEST HAIL	20 cm in diameter on 23 July 2010 in South Dakota, USA
LONGEST LIGHTNING BOLT	709 km on 31 October 2018 in Rio Grande do Sul, Brazil
COLDEST SUMMER	-33°C for July 2017 in Summit Camp, Greenland

DETAILS ABOUT
DARWIN

1 CHARLES DARWIN was a BRITISH NATURALIST who introduced the idea of EVOLUTION by NATURAL SELECTION in 1859 in his book 'On the Origin of Species'.

2 Darwin spent almost 5 years travelling ROUND THE WORLD on the ship HMS *Beagle*. On his voyage he observed ANIMAL SPECIES and collected FOSSILS.

3 Darwin studied FINCHES on the Galapagos Islands. He saw that birds' BEAKS ADAPTED into shapes that made it EASIER for them to PICK UP available food.

4 Darwin saw that animals of the SAME SPECIES were NOT EXACT COPIES of each other. Also, creatures were COMPETING for food, shelter and a mate.

5 If an animal has a difference that HELPS IT SURVIVE – such as being STRONGER, FASTER, SMARTER or MORE ATTRACTIVE – it's more likely to REPRODUCE and pass on its useful features.

6 Animals that aren't as well adapted to the world around them are LESS LIKELY TO SURVIVE.

7 Over MILLIONS OF YEARS, living things can CHANGE to suit new environments, creating completely NEW SPECIES. Or they can GO EXTINCT!

8 ADAPTATION is crucial to SURVIVAL. Most RABBITS have dark fur, but rabbits that live in SNOWY PLACES have adapted to having WHITE FUR as it gives them a higher chance of survival.

9 FIVE BILLION SPECIES have lived on Earth. 99% of them have DIED OUT.

10 Darwin helped to show that ALL LIVING THINGS ARE CONNECTED in a family tree that dates back billions of years to the beginning of LIFE ON EARTH.

EXTREME ELEMENTS

1
COPERNICIUM is a METAL that turns into a GAS at ROOM TEMPERATURE. So, in theory, you could breathe in metal.

2
ANTIMONY was used as a LAXATIVE for THOUSANDS OF YEARS. In fact, these PILLS were often RE-USED after passing through the body!

3
The rarest NATURALLY OCCURRING ELEMENT is ASTATINE. It is so RARE that there are only 28 GRAMS of astatine in the ENTIRE EARTH'S CRUST.

4
MERCURY is the only METAL that is LIQUID at ROOM TEMPERATURE. You can see it inside OLD THERMOMETERS.

5 BARIUM, CALCIUM, STRONTIUM, MAGNESIUM, CHLORINE, SODIUM, POTASSIUM and BORON have one thing in common – they were all first identified by SIR HUMPHRY DAVY.

6 The existence of TECHNETIUM was PREDICTED FOR 70 YEARS before it became the FIRST ELEMENT to be CREATED ARTIFICIALLY in a lab.

7 The HYDROGEN BOMB unleashed great DESTRUCTION when it was first tested in 1952. The nuclear explosion also created TWO NEW ELEMENTS – FERMIUM and EINSTEINIUM.

8 CHLORINE is a very POISONOUS GAS. SODIUM is a very POISONOUS METAL. Put them together and what do you get? ORDINARY TABLE SALT!

9 TENNESSINE is incredibly UNSTABLE and so SHORT-LIVED that scientists haven't even been able to work out whether it is a SOLID, LIQUID OR GAS!

10 CARBON has UNRIVALLED creative powers – there are more CARBON COMPOUNDS than compounds of all the other elements put together!

WAYS TO PROTECT THE PLANET

1 SAY NO TO PLASTIC STRAWS. They take **200 YEARS TO DECOMPOSE** and every year **5 BILLION ARE THROWN AWAY** in Britain.

2 PLANT A TREE. It will help the planet BREATHE!

3 RE-USE a METAL WATER BOTTLE rather than buying more plastic ones.

4 GIVE your OLD TOYS to YOUNGER CHILDREN – it will save buying them new ones!

5 START A GARDEN. Even if you only have a BALCONY, you could GROW HERBS to eat!

6 ADOPT AN ANIMAL. You could support TIGER CONSERVATION for just £3 A MONTH!

7 BEFRIEND THE BEES. Plant FLOWERS in your garden that they can POLLINATE – such as lavender, daisies and geraniums.

8 BUILD A BIRDHOUSE. With a few bits of WOOD and some GLUE, you could create a HAPPY HOME for a FAMILY OF BIRDS.

9 BIKE TO SCHOOL to cut down on POLLUTING CAR JOURNEYS.

10 EAT more LOCAL FOOD, rather than food that has flown halfway around the world to REACH YOUR PLATE!

Space

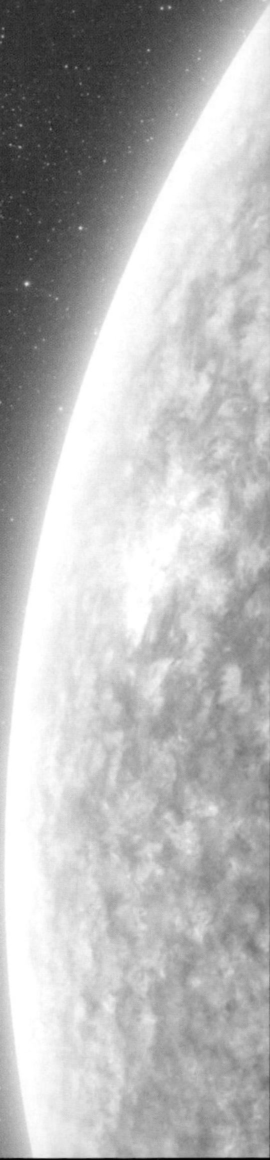

DID YOU KNOW?

It takes 8 minutes and 20 seconds for the light leaving the Sun to reach Earth!

Find more SCORCHING
SUN facts on page 142.

SOLAR SYSTEM STATS

1
MERCURY is **HOTTER** than your oven **IN THE DAY** (400°C) and **COLDER** than Antarctica **AT NIGHT** (-185°C) because it has **NO ATMOSPHERE** to keep heat in.

2
You would be **CRUSHED** instantly if you landed on **VENUS** – the **ATMOSPHERIC PRESSURE** on its surface is **92 TIMES** that **ON EARTH.**

3
All the **WATER** in Earth's **OCEANS** was carried here in the form of **ICY COMETS** that crashed into the young planet.

4
SATURN'S RINGS are 270,000 km in diameter but only 20 m deep. They are made of billions of **SHARDS OF ICE** and **ROCK.**

5 OLYMPUS MONS is a VOLCANO on MARS that is 3 times taller than MOUNT EVEREST. It is the tallest mountain on any planet in the Solar System.

6 A planet-sized OBJECT smacked into URANUS millions of years ago and KNOCKED IT onto its side, so now it ROLLS rather than spins.

7 JUPITER is 2.5 TIMES BIGGER than all the other planets in the Solar System put together. More than 1,300 EARTHS could FIT INSIDE the planet.

8 PLUTO was discovered in 1930 and called the ninth planet. In 2006 it was reclassified as a DWARF PLANET.

9 There could be as many as 120 DWARF PLANETS in our Solar System. They ORBIT in an area called the KUIPER BELT.

10 A YEAR on NEPTUNE is 165 EARTH YEARS LONG. Only 1 Neptunian year has passed since it was discovered!

SCORCHING SUN FACTS

1 The **SUN** is so **BIG** it could **SWALLOW** every other object in the Solar System – including **PLANETS, COMETS** and **ASTEROIDS.**

2 You could fit **1 MILLION EARTHS** into the **SUN.**

3 The Sun is **4.6 BILLION YEARS OLD.** It was born from a **NEBULA** – a cloud of dust and gas.

4 The Sun is a **BALL** of glowing **HOT GASES.** The **CORE** burns at **14 MILLION°C.**

5 **SUNSPOTS** are **COOLER AREAS** on the Sun's **SURFACE.** A sunspot formed in 2014 that was **130,000 KM WIDE.**

6 The Sun is **1.39 MILLION KM** in **DIAMETER.**

7 Sunlight is **EARTH'S PRIMARY ENERGY SOURCE.** It **WARMS US** in the day, powers our **WEATHER** and helps **PLANTS** grow.

8 Although it seems enormous to us, the Sun is only **AVERAGE IN SIZE** and **BRIGHTNESS** compared with **OTHER STARS.**

9 The **SUN'S CORE** is like a huge **NUCLEAR POWER STATION. HYDROGEN** gas fuses into **HELIUM**, releasing incredible amounts of **ENERGY.**

10 A **HYDROGEN BOMB** explodes with the power of **10 MILLION TONS** of TNT. The Sun releases **10 BILLION TIMES** this energy **EVERY SECOND!**

LARGEST
STARS

		NUMBER OF TIMES WIDER THAN THE SUN
1	UY Scuti	1,708
2	KY Cygni	1,420
3	AH Scorpii	1,411
4	Westerlund 1	1,241
5	BC Cygni	1,230
6	IRC-10414	1,200
7	PZ Cassiopeiae	1,190
8	V1489 Cygni	1,183
9	GCIRS 7	1,170
10	V766 Centauri	1,110

Did you know that the nine largest stars are all
BIGGER than the ENTIRE ORBIT OF JUPITER?

MAGICAL MOON FACTS

1 The **MOON ORBITS** the **EARTH** at a distance of **384,400 KM.** You could fit **ALL THE OTHER PLANETS** of the Solar System in **BETWEEN** Earth and the Moon!

2 **4.5 BILLION YEARS AGO** a **PLANET** the size of Mars **SMASHED INTO EARTH.** A **MOLTEN LUMP** of debris was **THROWN OUT** from the collision and over time this **BECAME THE MOON.**

3 The Moon is **3,476 KM** in **DIAMETER.** Relative to its planet, our moon is the **LARGEST SATELLITE** in the **SOLAR SYSTEM.**

4 The **MASS** of the Moon creates a **GRAVITATIONAL PULL** on our **OCEANS,** causing the **TIDES.**

5 We always **SEE THE SAME SIDE** of the Moon. It **TURNS ON ITS AXIS** in exactly the same time it takes to **ORBIT THE EARTH – 27.3 DAYS.**

6 The **DARK PATCHES** on the **MOON'S SURFACE** are known as seas, but actually they are huge, solidified **POOLS OF LAVA.**

7 The Moon seems to **SHINE BRIGHTLY,** but really its **SURFACE** is as **REFLECTIVE** as a **LUMP OF COAL.** It only seems bright compared with the **INKY DEPTHS OF SPACE** surrounding it!

8 **12 ASTRONAUTS** have **STEPPED ON** the **MOON'S SURFACE,** during the **6 APOLLO MISSIONS** that landed between 1969 and 1972. New moon missions are planned for later **THIS DECADE.**

9 **GRAVITY** on the Moon is **1/6 OF THAT ON EARTH.** Even wearing heavy spacesuits, astronauts were able to **SPRING LIKE GAZELLES** on the surface!

10 A **'BLUE MOON'** is when there are **TWO FULL MOONS** in **ONE CALENDAR MONTH.**

MOST MOONS

1	SATURN **83**	JUPITER **80**	**2**
3	URANUS **27**	NEPTUNE **14**	**4**
5	PLUTO **5**	MARS **2**	**6**
7	HAUMEA **2**	EARTH **1**	**8**
9	MERCURY **0**	VENUS **0**	**10**

Did you know that **PLUTO** and **HAUMEA** are **DWARF PLANETS?**

INTERNATIONAL SPACE STATION INSIGHTS

1 In just **24 HOURS**, the **INTERNATIONAL SPACE STATION** makes **16 ORBITS OF EARTH.**

2 There are a few **HOME COMFORTS** on board, including two **BATHROOMS**, one **GYM**, six **SLEEPING QUARTERS** and a 2-m-wide **VIEWING WINDOW.**

3 While on board, astronauts have to **EXERCISE** for **TWO HOURS EVERY DAY** to keep their muscles in shape.

4 The **LONGEST VISIT** to the ISS was by **PEGGY WHITSON**, who spent **665 DAYS** on board, setting the record on 3 September 2017.

5 The **LONGEST SPACEWALK** ever lasted for **8 HOURS** and **56 MINUTES** at the station in 2001.

6 As of 2021, **244 PEOPLE** have visited the ISS, representing **19 DIFFERENT COUNTRIES.**

7 The ISS orbits Earth at a height of **408 KM ABOVE THE PLANET'S SURFACE.**

8 **CONSTRUCTION** of the ISS began in **1998**. The **FIRST CREW** arrived in **NOVEMBER 2000.**

9 There are usually **7 CREW MEMBERS** on board the ISS at any one time.

10 Look up **AT NIGHT** and you can see the ISS. It's the **SECOND-BRIGHTEST OBJECT** in our night sky after the **MOON.**

ASTEROID FACTS

1. Asteroids are the rocky lumps of rubble left over from the Solar System's formation 4.6 billion years ago.

2. Asteroids are larger than 1 m across. Rocks smaller than this are called meteoroids.

3. Over 1 million asteroids larger than 1 km in diameter orbit the Sun in the Asteroid Belt.

4. Ceres is the largest asteroid at 940 km across. It is so large it is considered a dwarf planet.

5. The real Asteroid Belt isn't crowded as it is in films. The average distance between rocks is more than 1.2 million km!

6. Asteroids can be knocked from their orbit by collisions. Then they can tumble off towards Earth.

7. More than 1,000 people were injured when a 19-m-wide asteroid exploded into pieces above Chelyabinsk, Russia, in 2013.

8. Every planet in the Solar System has been smashed by asteroids (and the occasional comet).

9. Not all asteroid strikes are bad. Some rocks contain organic compounds that may have kickstarted life on Earth!

10. Astronomers scan the skies for space rocks, hoping to give us plenty of warning!

BIGGEST CRATER COLLISIONS

		YEARS AGO	DIAMETER
1	Vredefort Crater, South Africa	2 billion	300 km
2	Chicxulub Crater, Mexico	65 million	180 km
3	Sudbury Basin, Canada	1.8 billion	130 km
4	Woodleigh Crater, Australia	364 million	60–160 km
5	Manicouagan Crater, Canada	215 million	100 km
6	Acraman Crater, Australia	580 million	90 km
7	Popigai Crater, Russia	35.7 million	90 km
8	Chesapeake Bay Crater, USA	35 million	85 km
9	Morokweng Crater, South Africa	145 million	70 km
10	Kara Crater, Russia	70.3 million	65 km

MOST ADVENTUROUS ASTRONAUTS

1 In 1961, **YURI GAGARIN** became the **FIRST HUMAN BEING IN SPACE** when he made one orbit of the Earth.

2 **NEIL ARMSTRONG** became the **FIRST HUMAN** to step **ON THE MOON** on **21 JULY 1969**.

3 The **FIRST AMERICAN** to orbit the Earth was **JOHN GLENN** in **1962**. He also became the **OLDEST EVER ASTRONAUT** 37 years later.

4 Cosmonaut **VALENTINA TERESHKOVA** was the **FIRST WOMAN** in space in **1963** aboard the Vostok 6.

5 Astronaut **SCOTT KELLY** spent a year in orbit while his **IDENTICAL TWIN BROTHER MARK** stayed on Earth – to see how much a **HUMAN BODY CHANGES IN SPACE**. Scott grew **2 INCHES TALLER** than Mark while in space!

6 **APOLLO 13** suffered an **EXPLOSION** heading to the Moon – **JIM LOVELL** was the cool commander who brought it **SAFELY HOME**.

7 The first person to make an **UNTETHERED SPACEWALK** was **BRUCE MCCANDLESS** in **1984**. He floated free for **6 HOURS 17 MINUTES!**

8 **OLIVER DAEMEN** became the **YOUNGEST EVER** person in space when he flew on Blue Origin NS-16 **AT THE AGE OF 18!**

9 **LAIKA** the dog was the **FIRST ANIMAL** to orbit the Earth.

10 **JERRY ROSS** and **FRANKLIN DIAZ** share the record for **MOST LAUNCHES** to orbit – **7!**

STRANGEST SPACE OBJECTS

1 Mysterious radio signals come from billions of light years away and have mystified astronomers!

2 'Oumuamua' was a kilometre-long space object that shot into, and back out of, our Solar System. No one is exactly sure what it was!

3 A 'moonmoon' is a moon that orbits another moon!

4 Flung away from their star, rogue planets drift through the galaxy.

5 The stringy remains of a dead star, called nuclear pasta, is the strongest substance in the universe —10 billion times stronger than steel.

6 Neutron star is the densest material in the universe— a teaspoonful would weigh 1 trillion kg!

7 There are two fermi bubbles at the centre of our galaxy— colossal blobs 50,000 light years across, filled with very hot gas and cosmic rays.

8 Tabby's star dips in brightness because it is surrounded by huge gas clouds.

9 Saturn's moon Hyperion is charged with a 'particle beam' of static electricity that flows out into space.

10 Astronomers think there might be an undiscovered planet in our own Solar System, Planet 9, that would be 10 times bigger than Earth and 200 times farther from the Sun.

LARGEST OPTICAL TELESCOPES

		LOCATION	SIZE
1	Gran Telescopio Canarias	Canary Islands	10.4 m
2	Hobby-Eberly Telescope	Texas, USA	10 m
3	Keck Telescope	Hawaii, USA	10 m
4	South African Large Telescope	South Africa	10 m
5	Large Binocular Telescope	Arizona, USA	8.4 m
6	Subaru Telescope	Hawaii, USA	8.2 m
7	Very Large Telescope	Chile	8.2 m
8	Gemini North & South	Hawaii & Chile	8.1 m
9	MMT Observatory	Arizona, USA	6.5 m
10	Magellan 1 & 2	Chile	6.5 m

Human World

DID YOU KNOW?

The Great Wall of China took more than 2,000 years to build!

Find more LUDICROUS LANDMARK facts on page 198.

COOLEST CASTLES

1 Neuschwanstein Palace, Germany

With its dreamy turrets and spires, this impressive building was the inspiration for the Disneyland castle!

This castle is a strategic masterpiece with 8 huge towers, 2 barbicans and sheer stone walls.

2 Conwy Castle, Wales

3 Predjama Castle, Slovenia

It looks as if it has been carved directly out of a cliff face, but this castle is actually built in the mouth of a cave.

Built on a rocky isle where three lochs meet, with towering hills in the background, this is the ultimate Scottish castle.

4 Eilean Donan Castle, Scotland

5 Windsor Castle, England

Home sweet home to the British Royal Family, this is the longest-occupied and largest palace in the world.

Lying deep in the heart of Transylvania, this spooky building has earned the nickname 'Dracula's Castle'!

6 Bran Castle, Romania

7

This is an unusual fortress because it is so brightly coloured!

Pena Castle, Portugal

8

Alcázar of Segovia, Spain

Spectacularly designed to look like the prow of a ship, this castle has also been a prison, a palace and a college!

9 De Haar Castle, Netherlands

Packed with over 200 rooms, this fortress is surrounded by magnificent moats, lakes and gardens.

10 Tower of London, England

Home to the priceless CROWN JEWELS of THE UNITED KINGDOM, the TOWER was also a prison in the past.

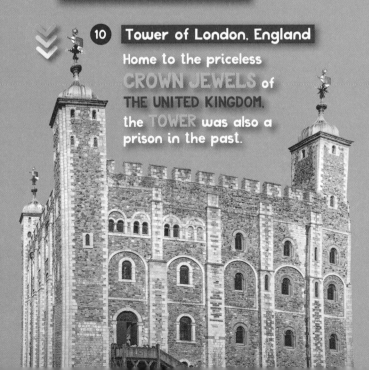

WEIRDEST WORLD CHAMPIONSHIPS

1 PEASHOOTING, ENGLAND

Blow peas through a straw and try to hit the target!

2 SNAIL RACING, ENGLAND

The snails start in the centre of a circular track—first to the edge wins. Ready, steady, slow!

3 POOH STICKS, ENGLAND

Contestants drop brightly coloured sticks off one side of a bridge, then race to the other.

4 AIR GUITAR, FINLAND

You don't need a real instrument to rock the world—just pretend!

5 STINGING NETTLE EATING, ENGLAND

Scoff as many stinging nettles as you can in one hour—if you can stomach it!

6 WELLY WANGING, ENGLAND

How far can you wang (Yorkshire for throw) your welly boot?

7 STONE SKIMMING, SCOTLAND

How many times can you make a stone skip across a pond?

8 ROCK PAPER SCISSORS, WORLDWIDE

This is a professional game of speed and skill. Some experts even research winning strategies!

9 BOG SNORKELLING, WALES

Swim under the murky water with a facemask and a breathing tube, as fast as you can!

10 EXTREME IRONING, WORLDWIDE

This means ironing in extreme locations—up a mountain, on a speeding car, even underwater!

FREAKIEST FOODS

1 DURIAN FRUIT

The durian fruit is known for its strong odour. Some people think it smells like rotten onions, or even raw sewage!

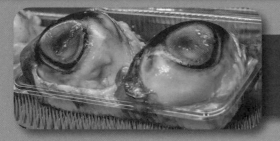

2 TUNA EYEBALLS

Would you dare to eat the eyeballs of this giant fish?

3 FRIED TARANTULAS

These giant spiders are scary enough when they're alive – how about on a stick?

4 HÁKARL

This is the rotting, fermented carcass of a shark – but it's a delicacy in Iceland!

5 CHICKEN FEET

Chicken feet are cooked and eaten in many countries.

6 100-YEAR-OLD EGG

The egg is preserved in ash until the yolk turns green and the white transforms into slimy brown jelly.

7 GRASSHOPPERS

These insects are seasoned with salt, pepper and chilli, and cooked in a big wok.

8 BIRD'S NEST SOUP

The swiftlet bird uses its own sticky saliva instead of twigs to build its nest – then people use the nest to make soup!

9 FROGS' LEGS

Frogs' legs can be grilled, baked, fried or stewed. Apparently they have the texture of chicken and taste like fish.

10 CASU MARTZU

This is known as 'maggot cheese' because it is served with live insect larvae happily burrowing through the cheese itself.

BIZARRE BUILDINGS

1 Crazy House, Vietnam

Inspired by fairy tales and built to look like a giant tree, this house certainly lives up to its name.

2 The walls of this chapel are completely covered in human skulls and bones!

Capella dos Ossos, Portugal

Little Crooked House, Poland

4 This bendy building looks like it has been reflected in a fairground mirror.

3

The Million Bottle Temple, Thailand

This Buddhist temple is made entirely from discarded beer bottles.

This shoe-shaped house was built for a successful shoe salesman in the 1940s – and was modelled on one of his own work boots.

Everything in this house is topsy-turvy – even the furniture is on the ceiling!

5

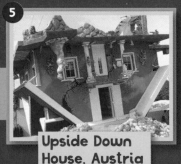

Upside Down House, Austria

6

The Haines Shoe House, USA

7

This 26-m tall office building looks exactly like a shopping basket – complete with handles.

Basket Building, USA

8

Horace Burgess's Treehouse, USA

The world's largest treehouse was 30 m tall and was spread across 7 huge oak trees.

9

Kansas City Library, USA

The front of this building looks like a bookshelf – with 8-m high books!

10 **The Square Head, France**

This habitable SCULPTURE houses a 30-m LIBRARY of 7 floors – 3 in the NECK and 4 in the CUBE that makes up the HEAD.

TALLEST BUILDINGS

1 BURJ KHALIFA – 828 M

Located in Dubai, UAE, this astonishing building (pictured) has been the **TALLEST STRUCTURE IN THE WORLD** since 2009.

2 MERDEKA 118 – 679 M

This tower in Kuala Lumpur, Malaysia, gets its name from the **MALAY WORD for 'FREEDOM'** – and from its **118 STOREYS!**

3 SHANGHAI TOWER – 632 M

In Shanghai, China, you can visit the **WORLD'S HIGHEST OBSERVATION DECK** at **562 M.**

4 ABRAJ AL-BAIT CLOCK TOWER – 601 M

This building in Mecca, Saudi Arabia, has seven hotels and the **WORLD'S LARGEST CLOCK FACE** at **43 M** in diameter.

5 PING AN INTERNATIONAL FINANCE CENTER – 599 M

In Shenzhen, China, you'll find this 115-storey building with **33 DOUBLE-DECKER LIFTS!**

6 LOTTE WORLD TOWER – 555 M

South Korea's tallest building is in the capital city, Seoul. It took **13 YEARS TO PLAN** and **7 YEARS TO CONSTRUCT!**

7 ONE WORLD TRADE CENTER – 541 M

With 94 storeys, this New York landmark is the **TALLEST BUILDING IN THE USA** and the **WESTERN HEMISPHERE.**

8 GUANGZHOU CTF FINANCE CENTRE – 530 M

The Centre in Guangzhou, China, has the **FASTEST LIFTS IN THE WORLD** – you can shoot 440 m to the **95TH FLOOR** in **JUST 42 SECONDS!**

9 TIANJIN CTF FINANCE CENTRE – 530 M

Found in Tianjin, China, this tower's **CURVING SHAPE** was designed to help it **WITHSTAND EARTHQUAKES.**

10 CHINA ZUN – 528 M

This building in Beijing, China, got its **NAME** – 'zun' – and **SHAPE** from an **ANCIENT CHINESE WINE GLASS!**

TALLEST STATUES

1	**STATUE OF UNITY** India **182 m**	**SPRING TEMPLE BUDDHA** China **128 m**	**2**
3	**LAYKYUN SEKKYA** MYANMAR **116 m**	**STATUE OF BELIEF** India **106 m**	**4**
5	**USHIKU DAIBUTSU** Japan **100 m**	**SENDAI DAIKANNON** Japan **100 m**	**6**
7	**GUISHAN GUANYIN** China **99 m**	**GREAT BUDDHA OF THAILAND** Thailand **92 m**	**8**
9	**DAI KANNON OF KITA NO MIYAKO PARK** Japan **88 m**	**MOTHER OF ALL ASIA – TOWER OF PEACE** Philippines **88 m**	**10**

Did you know that the **STATUE OF LIBERTY** in **NEW YORK** is only the **51ST-TALLEST STATUE** in the world at **46 M HIGH?**

BRILLIANT BRIDGES

) ÇANAKKALE 1915 BRIDGE, TURKEY

Opened in 2022, this is the longest suspension bridge in the world, at 4.6 km long.

2 ZHANGJIAJIE GLASS BRIDGE, CHINA

Would you dare to cross the highest and longest glass bridge in the world? It spans a 300-m gorge!

3 GOLDEN GATE BRIDGE, USA

The most-photographed bridge in the world was also the longest when it opened in 1937.

4 MILLAU VIADUCT, FRANCE

This is the world's tallest bridge, at 336.4 m high.

5 FORTH BRIDGE, SCOTLAND

This is one of the world's biggest cantilever bridges and a Scottish landmark.

6 SYDNEY HARBOUR BRIDGE, AUSTRALIA

You can actually climb this famous bridge!

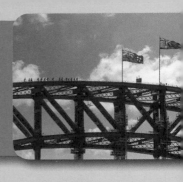

7 RIALTO BRIDGE, VENICE

This beautiful bridge built in 1591 is lined with shops.

8 STARI MOST, BOSNIA

It's traditional for local youngsters to jump off this bridge – 24 m into the river!

9 PONT DU GARD, FRANCE

This triple-decker aqueduct was built by the Romans and is still standing today.

10 TOWER BRIDGE, LONDON

This Victorian bridge is an instant icon of a famous city.

STUNNING STADIUMS

Camp Nou, Spain

99,000 football fans fill these stands to watch Barcelona, making this one of the largest stadiums in the world.

San Siro, Italy

Seating 80,000 fans, this huge stadium in Milan is shared by fierce rivals – Inter and AC Milan.

Michigan Stadium, USA

The third largest stadium in the world is home to the University of Michigan's American football team, with a capacity of 107,601.

Maracana, Brazil

This stadium held a world-record-breaking 199,854 spectators for the 1950 World Cup final.

Not only is this stadium shaped like a dragon, its roof has 8,844 solar panels that generate enough electricity to run the stadium.

Bird's Nest Stadium, China

This beautiful stadium has a lattice of steel beams that make it look like a colossal nest.

National Stadium, Taiwan

7

Wembley's landmark 134-m-high arch is the world's longest unsupported roof structure.

Wembley, UK

8

Arthur Ashe Stadium, USA

This is the largest tennis stadium in the world and has 23,771 seats.

9 Indianapolis Motor Speedway, USA

With the largest capacity of any sports venue in the world, this motorsport mecca can hold 257,325 fans.

10 Beijing National Aquatics Centre, China

Known as the WATER CUBE, this SHIMMERING STADIUM is made up of 4,000 PIECES of very strong plastic.

YOUNGEST SPORTS CHAMPIONS

1 Aged **17**, **PELÉ** became the **YOUNGEST-EVER FOOTBALLER** to play in a **WORLD CUP FINAL**. He scored **2 GOALS** as Brazil beat Sweden 5–2 in 1958.

2 In 1976, **14-YEAR-OLD NADIA COMĂNECI** was the **FIRST GYMNAST** to be awarded a **PERFECT SCORE** of 10.0 at the Olympic Games.

3 **MARJORIE GESTRING** is the **YOUNGEST PERSON** ever to win an **OLYMPIC GOLD MEDAL.** She was **JUST 13** when she won the 3 m springboard diving title at the 1936 games in Munich, Germany.

4 The **YOUNGEST BOXER** ever to win a **HEAVYWEIGHT TITLE** is **MIKE TYSON,** who was only **20** when he triumphed in this very tough sport.

5 **FERNANDO ALONSO** first drove a racing kart when he was only three. He became a **FORMULA 1 DRIVER** aged **19.**

6 **RONNIE O'SULLIVAN** made his **FIRST CENTURY BREAK** in **SNOOKER** aged **TEN.** He turned professional at 16 and **WON** his first tournament a year later.

7 **JAHANGIR KHAN** is the **GREATEST SQUASH PLAYER** of all time. He **WON** the **WORLD AMATEUR** title aged 15, and the **WORLD OPEN** aged **17.**

8 **IAN THORPE** swam for Australia aged only 14. Aged **17,** he was the **MOST SUCCESSFUL ATHLETE** at the **2000 OLYMPIC GAMES,** with three golds, two silvers and three world records.

9 In 1985, **17-YEAR-OLD BORIS BECKER** became the first unseeded player ever to **WIN WIMBLEDON,** and the **YOUNGEST MALE CHAMPION.**

MARTINA HINGIS entered her first tennis competition aged four! In 1996, she became the **YOUNGEST GRAND SLAM CHAMPION** of all time at **15 YEARS OLD.**

MOST POPULAR SPORTS

1

FOOTBALL
4 billion fans

2

CRICKET
2.5 billion fans

3

HOCKEY
2 billion fans

4

TENNIS
1 billion fans

5

VOLLEYBALL
900 million fans

6

TABLE TENNIS
875 million fans

7

BASKETBALL
825 million fans

8

BASEBALL
500 million fans

9

RUGBY
475 million fans

10

GOLF
450 million fans

DID YOU KNOW THAT THE FIFA WORLD CUP IS THE WORLD'S MOST-WATCHED SPORTING EVENT? AROUND 3.5 BILLION PEOPLE TUNED IN TO THE 2018 TOURNAMENT.

MOST POPULAR VIDEO GAMES

	RELEASED	SALES
1 MINECRAFT	2011	238 million
2 GRAND THEFT AUTO V	2013	165 million
3 TETRIS	1989	100 million
4 WII SPORTS	2006	83 million
5 BATTLEGROUNDS	2017	75 million
6 SUPER MARIO BROS.	1985	58 million
7 MARIO KART 8	2014	55 million
8 POKÉMON	1996	48 million
9 TERRARIA	2011	45 million
10 RED DEAD REDEMPTION 2	2018	44 million

DID YOU KNOW THAT ONE DAY IN MINECRAFT IS 20 MINUTES IN REAL TIME? IF OUR DAYS WERE THAT SHORT, A YEAR WOULD TAKE JUST OVER 5 DAYS!

WACKIEST RACES

1 PACK BURRO RACING, USA

'Burros' (Spanish for donkeys) might look quiet and lazy, but they love to run!

2 CANE TOAD RACING, AUSTRALIA

Pick your toad, kiss it for luck, put it in the middle of the table, then hope your amphibian is the first to jump off the table!

4 PANTOMIME HORSE GRAND NATIONAL, ENGLAND

This is just like the proper Grand National... but the horses are people in costumes!

3 COCKROACH RACING, AUSTRALIA

Another Aussie favourite—the first roach across the finish line is the winner!

5 DRONE RACING, WORLDWIDE

If you're a skilled drone pilot, then this is the race for you.

6

KETTLE-HEAD KILOMETRE, SCOTLAND

Securely strap a kettle to your head, then be the first to complete the 1-km obstacle course.

7 ## BED RACING, USA

Team members huff and puff as they shove a bed at high speed – with one lucky person getting to lie in it!

8

KRISPY KREME CHALLENGE, USA

Here's a tasty challenge – run 2.5 miles to the Krispy Kreme doughnut shop, scoff 12 doughnuts, then run back to the start.

LAWNMOWER RACING, WORLDWIDE

They aren't normally known for their speed, but these lawnmowers have been souped up and turned into racing machines!

10 ## MOUNTAIN UNICYCLING, CANADA

Climbing mountains is hard enough – how about doing it on a unicycle?

HAIR-RAISING
ROLLERCOASTERS

FORMULA ROSSA, ABU DHABI

1 The fastest rollercoaster in the world launches you at 240 km/h.

KINGDA KA, USA

2 The world's tallest rollercoaster climbs to 139 m – higher than the dome of St Paul's Cathedral – then drops straight down!

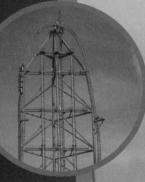

TMNT SHELLRAISER, USA

3 The world's steepest rollercoaster has a head-spinning drop angle of 121.5°!

SMILER, ENGLAND

4 Don't eat before you ride this one – it has 14 inversions with rolls, loops and corkscrews.

BANSHEE, USA

5 The world's longest inverted rollercoaster screams along for 1.26 km and reaches 110 km/h!

LEAP-THE-DIPS, USA

6 This is scary because it looks ancient! It opened in 1902 and is the world's oldest rollercoaster.

LEGENDARY TWIN DRAGON, CHINA

7 The highest inverted rollercoaster climbs to 70 m in the air. It's fast too, at 119 km/h.

WILDFIRE, SWEDEN

8 The world's highest wooden rollercoaster climbs to 56 m and flips you upside down three times!

SHOCK WAVE, USA

9 Back-to-back loops generate 5.9 G of acceleration.

STEEL DRAGON 2000, JAPAN

10

The longest **ROLLERCOASTER** in the **WORLD** covers **2.48 KM** in just **4 MINUTES!**

SUPERCOOL SUPERCARS

1 MCLAREN F1

When it launched in 1992, no other road car came close to the F1's 231 mph top speed.

2 BUGATTI VEYRON 16.4 SUPER SPORT

With a top speed of 268 mph, this is now the fastest supercar in the world.

3 ASTON MARTIN ONE-77

Only 77 of these exclusive 200-mph hypercars were ever built.

4 KOENIGSEGG CCXR

The CCXR is the world's first green supercar! It creates 1,018 horsepower using biofuel.

ONE-77

5 FORD GT

In 2005 Ford made a retro-looking supercar to honour their great GT40 model that dominated the Le Mans race in the 1960s.

6 PORSCHE CARRERA GT

You'll hear this supercar coming before you see it – the 5.7-litre V-8 creates 603 horsepower.

7 TESLA ROADSTER

This electric speed machine accelerates from 0–60 mph in just 1.9 seconds!

8 LAMBORGHINI HURACÁN

This flying wedge of a car has a 10-cylinder engine and a top speed of 201 mph.

9 PAGANI ZONDA

The exotic design of this supercar was inspired by jet fighters.

10 FERRARI ENZO

Packing 651 horsepower, this supercar was named after the company's founder.

FASTEST VEHICLES

MANNED SPACECRAFT
Record: 39,897 km/h in 1969
Apollo 10

FIGHTER JET
Record: 3,494 km/h in 1970
MiG-25 Foxbat

PASSENGER AIRLINER
Record: 2,430 km/h in 1968
Tupolev Tu-144

LAND SPEED
Record: 1,228 km/h in 1997
ThrustSSC

TRAIN
Record: 603 km/h in 2015
Maglev train

BOAT
Record: 511 km/h in 1978
Spirit of Australia

PRODUCTION CAR
Record: 447 km/h in 2017
Koenigsegg Agera RS

MOTORCYCLE
Record: 399 km/h in 1999
Suzuki Hayabusa

HELICOPTER
Record: 315 km/h in 2007
CH-47F Chinook

SUBMARINE
Record: 44.7 knots (82.8 km/h) in 1969
K-222

DID YOU KNOW THAT APOLLO 10 WAS THE 'DRESS REHEARSAL' FOR THE FIRST MOON LANDING? THE SPACECRAFT SET THE RECORD FOR THE HIGHEST SPEED ATTAINED BY A CREWED VEHICLE ON 26 MAY 1969 DURING ITS RETURN FROM SPACE.

BIGGEST SHIPS

		TONNAGE	LENGTH
1	PIONEERING SPIRIT (CRANE VESSEL)	403,342	382 m
2	BELLAMYA (SUPERTANKER)	275,276	414 m
3	FSO ASIA (SUPERTANKER)	236,638	379 m
4	CMA CGM JACQUES SAADÉ (CONTAINER SHIP)	236,583	400 m
5	WONDER OF THE SEAS (CRUISE SHIP)	236,857	362 m
6	YUAN HE HAI (ORE CARRIER)	203,403	362 m
7	GERALD R. FORD (AIRCRAFT CARRIER)	100,000	333 m
8	RMS QUEEN MARY 2 (OCEAN LINER)	148,528	345 m
9	RMS TITANIC (OCEAN LINER)	46,328	269 m
10	CLUB MED 2 (SAILING SHIP)	14,983	194 m

DID YOU KNOW THAT THE PIONEERING SPIRIT IS THE SIZE OF TWO SUPERTANKERS WITH AN AREA THE SIZE OF EIGHT FOOTBALL FIELDS?

TASTY PIZZA FACTS

1
PIZZA was INVENTED in NAPLES, ITALY, around 200 YEARS AGO.

2
Pizza was SPREAD AROUND THE WORLD – particularly in NEW YORK, USA – by ITALIAN EMIGRANTS IN THE 20TH CENTURY.

3
The classic MARGHERITA PIZZA was first created for QUEEN MARGHERITA OF ITALY in 1889, using MOZZARELLA, TOMATOES AND BASIL to represent the ITALIAN FLAG – white, red and green!

4
The BIGGEST-EVER PIZZA was the size of FIVE TENNIS COURTS It measured 1,261.65 m² and was prepared in ROME, ITALY, in 2012.

5
The ORIGINAL ITALIAN PIZZAS were SQUARE in shape.

6
New Zealander Josh Anderson ate a whole 12-INCH PIZZA in JUST 1 MINUTE and 45 SECONDS!

7
5 BILLION PIZZAS are sold EVERY YEAR! That's 9,500 EVERY SINGLE MINUTE.

8
HAWAIIAN PIZZA was actually invented in CANADA by a GREEK CHEF! Sam Panopoulos, a cook in Ontario, first added TINNED PINEAPPLE to a pizza in 1962.

9
SQUID is the most popular PIZZA TOPPING in JAPAN. In the UK and the USA, PEPPERONI is the TOP TOPPING!

10
In 2001, the FIRST PIZZA was DELIVERED TO OUTER SPACE when Pizza Hut delivered a 6-inch salami pizza to the INTERNATIONAL SPACE STATION!

MOST MONSTROUS
FRUIT & VEG

1 The **WORLD'S HEAVIEST PUMPKIN** weighed 1,190 KG, which is **OVER A TONNE.** Imagine carving that!

2 The **WORLD'S HEAVIEST LEMON** weighed 5.3 KG. It was 74 cm in circumference and 35 cm high!

3 A CARROT weighing 10.17 KG was grown in Minnesota, USA, in 2017.

4 An 8.5-KG ONION was grown in the UK in 2014 – chop that without crying!

5 A man from Nottinghamshire, UK, grew a **CAULIFLOWER** in 2014 that weighed 27.48 KG.

6 The **WORLD'S LONGEST LEEK**, grown by Joe Atherton in the UK, measured 1.36 M!

7 The **HEAVIEST APPLE** weighed 1.8 KG, grown by Chisato Iwasaki at his apple farm in Japan in 2005.

8 A **POTATO** weighing 4.98 KG claimed the world record in 2011.

9 The **WORLD'S HEAVIEST BROCCOLI** weighed 15.87 KG and was grown in Alaska, USA, in 1993.

10 The **LARGEST BUNCH** of bananas ever grown contained **473 INDIVIDUAL BANANAS,** weighing in at 130 KG!

185

STRANGEST SUPERSTITIONS

1

Beginner's luck

If you try a sport or game for the first time and beat an expert, that's beginner's luck.

2

Sleeping in make-up

If you visit Vietnam, neve sleep with make-up on. Demons will think you are one of them!

3

Birds looking in

If a bird peers in your window in France, it means that something bad will happen soon.

4

Many Chinese buildings don't have a fourth floor. The character for 'four' sounds like the character for 'death' in Chinese, and is bad luck.

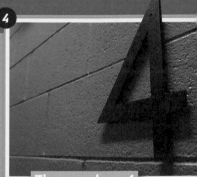

The number 4

5

In some Kenyan villages, locals believe that geese only quack at witches!

Geese quacking

6

You do this to ward off bad luck. The idea comes from myths about good spirits living in trees.

Touch wood

7

Ladders

Superstition says it's bad luck to walk under ladders. Actually, it's just sensible!

8

Friday the 13th

The fear of Friday the 13th is known as friggatriskaidekaphobia!

9

Scissors

Don't hand scissors to someone in Turkey – it means you will become enemies.

10

Breaking a mirror

This brings **7 YEARS** of bad luck. It comes from the belief that **MIRRORS** don't just reflect your image, they hold bits of your soul.

MYTHICAL MONSTERS

1 Vampires are blood-sucking beasts that come out at night to prey on humans.

2 Slender man has only been around since 2009, but this unnaturally tall, faceless creature has done plenty of scaring already!

3 Mylings jump on the backs of travellers and demand to be taken to the graveyard – growing bigger on the way, so the victim sinks into the soil!

4 Djinns are demons that are mentioned in the Quran and were created from a smokeless and scorching fire.

5 Pontianaks are evil creatures from Malaysia with long black hair and red eyes, wearing white dresses smeared with blood.

6 The Mothman is a frightening creature with 3-m-wide wings and glowing red eyes.

7 Sirens are monsters that appear as beautiful women to lure passing sailors to their death on the rocks.

8 Weeping angels are the scary statues from *Doctor Who* that sneak up on you when you close your eyes!

9 The Jiangshi is a green-skinned zombie from China that kills living creatures to absorb their life force.

WEREWOLVES look like ordinary **HUMANS** most of the time, but they transform into **GIANT WOLVES** at the full **MOON!**

10

EERIEST ABANDONED PLACES

1 BEELITZ HOSPITAL, GERMANY

This spooky old sanatorium is lost on the edge of a forest.

2 PRIPYAT, UKRAINE

This entire town was evacuated when the nuclear reactor at nearby Chernobyl exploded in 1986.

3 RED SANDS SEA FORTS, ENGLAND

These alien-looking fortresses were built as lookout posts in the Thames estuary. They were later used by a pirate radio station!

4 HASHIMA ISLAND, JAPAN

This coal-mining island was once the most densely populated place on Earth; now it resembles a derelict warship.

5 ORPHEUM THEATRE, USA

This theatre in Massachusetts was opened on the same day the *Titanic* hit an iceberg.

6 ST KILDA, SCOTLAND

In 1930, the residents of the UK's most remote islands decided to leave for the mainland, never to return.

7 SAN JUAN PARANGARICUTIRO, MEXICO

This church tower is all that remains of the village of San Juan Parangaricutiro, which was devastated by a volcano.

8 ATHENS OLYMPIC VENUES, GREECE

Sadly, many of the sports venues were not re-used after the 2004 Olympics, and now they are falling to pieces.

10 STAR WARS SET, TUNISIA

The original set of the desert planet in *Star Wars* was simply abandoned in the desert. It was found years later on Google Earth!

9 ROSS ISLAND, ANTARCTICA

The supply base for explorer Captain Scott was abandoned when he died on his attempt to reach the South Pole.

COUNTRIES & CITIES

BIGGEST COUNTRIES

1	Russia	17,075,400 km²
2	Canada	9,984,670 km²
3	USA	9,826,635 km²
4	China	9,606,802 km²
5	Brazil	8,514,879 km²
6	Australia	7,692,024 km²
7	India	3,166,620 km²
8	Argentina	2,776,889 km²
9	Kazakhstan	2,717,300 km²
10	Algeria	2,381,741 km²

SMALLEST COUNTRIES

1	Vatican City	0.5 km²
2	Monaco	2 km²
3	Nauru	21 km²
4	Tuvalu	25 km²
5	San Marino	61 km²
6	Liechtenstein	160 km²
7	Marshall Islands	181 km²
8	St Kitts and Nevis	261 km²
9	Maldives	298 km²
10	Malta	316 km²

COUNTRIES WITH MOST PEOPLE

1	China	1,411,860,295
2	India	1,366,417,756
3	USA	329,064,917
4	Indonesia	270,625,567
5	Pakistan	216,565,317
6	Brazil	211,049,519
7	Nigeria	200,963,603
8	Bangladesh	163,046,173
9	Russia	145,872,260
10	Mexico	127,575,529

CITIES WITH MOST PEOPLE

1	Tokyo, Japan (below)	37,393,129
2	Delhi, India	30,290,936
3	Shanghai, China	27,058,479
4	São Paulo, Brazil	22,043,028
5	Mexico City, Mexico	21,782,378
6	Dhaka, Bangladesh	21,005,860
7	Cairo, Egypt	20,900,604
8	Beijing, China	20,462,610
9	Mumbai, India	20,411,274
10	Osaka, Japan	19,165,340

FACTS ABOUT FLAGS

1 There are three national flags that are different on the front and the back – Moldova, Paraguay and Saudi Arabia.

2 The only country with a flag that is not a rectangle or square is Nepal. The Nepalese flag is made of two stacked triangles to represent the Himalaya mountains.

3 Only two countries have square flags. Switzerland's flag has a white cross on a red background. The Vatican City flag is white and yellow with a design of two crossed keys.

4 Denmark's flag – a white cross on a red background – has been used since 1219 and is the oldest in the world.

5 When the Queen is staying at Buckingham Palace, the Royal Standard is flown. When she leaves the palace, the Union Jack is flown instead.

6 The flag of Belize has 12 colours on it, the most of any country.

7 Purple is the rarest colour in national flags – only Nicaragua and Dominica feature it.

8 Several countries feature religious symbols on their flags. Turkey has the crescent and star of Islam. Israel has the star of David. Scotland features the cross of St Andrew.

9 The biggest-ever flag was three times the size of a football pitch! This Romanian monster flag measured 349 × 227 m, weighed five tonnes, and took 200 people several hours to unfurl.

The **STUDY** of **FLAGS** and their **HISTORY** is called **VEXILLOLOGY**.

10

BUSIEST INTERNATIONAL AIRPORTS

1 **DUBAI INTERNATIONAL AIRPORT**
Dubai, UAE
86,328,896 passengers

2 **AMSTERDAM AIRPORT SCHIPHOL**
Amsterdam, Netherlands
76,043,973 passengers

3 **LONDON HEATHROW AIRPORT**
London, UK
71,679,691 passengers

4 **HONG KONG INTERNATIONAL AIRPORT**
Hong Kong, China
71,287,552 passengers

5 **SEOUL INCHEON INTERNATIONAL AIRPORT**
Seoul, South Korea
70,578,050 passengers

6 **PARIS CHARLES DE GAULLE AIRPORT**
Paris, France
69,823,084 passengers

7 **SINGAPORE CHANGI AIRPORT**
Singapore
67,601,000 passengers

8 **FRANKFURT AIRPORT**
Frankfurt, Germany
63,067,739 passengers

9 **SUVARNABHUMI AIRPORT**
Bangkok, Thailand
52,933,565 passengers

10 **TAOYUAN INTERNATIONAL AIRPORT**
Taipei, Taiwan
48,360,290 passengers

DID YOU KNOW THAT DUBAI INTERNATIONAL AIRPORT HAS ITS OWN FIVE-STAR HOTEL WITHIN THE TERMINAL 1 BUILDING? GUESTS CAN ESCAPE THE CROWDS AND ENJOY THE LUXURY FACILITIES!

LARGEST METRO SYSTEMS

		NO. OF STATIONS	YEAR OPENED
1	NEW YORK CITY SUBWAY, USA	424	1904
2	SHANGHAI METRO, CHINA	345	1993
3	BEIJING SUBWAY, CHINA	331	1969
4	SEOUL METRO, SOUTH KOREA	315	1974
5	PARIS METRO, FRANCE	303	1900
6	MADRID METRO, SPAIN	302	1919
7	LONDON UNDERGROUND, UK	272	1863
8	GUANGZHOU METRO, CHINA	257	1997
9	MOSCOW METRO, RUSSIA	236	1935
10	DELHI METRO, INDIA	229	2002

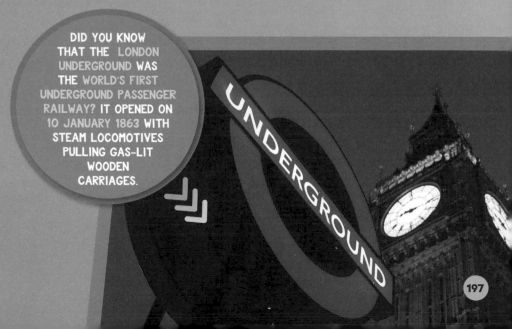

DID YOU KNOW THAT THE LONDON UNDERGROUND WAS THE WORLD'S FIRST UNDERGROUND PASSENGER RAILWAY? IT OPENED ON 10 JANUARY 1863 WITH STEAM LOCOMOTIVES PULLING GAS-LIT WOODEN CARRIAGES.

LUDICROUS LANDMARKS

1 BIG BEN

'Big Ben' is the name of the bell that hangs in London's famous clock tower. The 96-m-tall building itself is officially called the Elizabeth Tower!

2 PYRAMIDS

The Pyramids in Egypt used to be even more stunning than they are now – they were originally covered in smooth white limestone.

4 EIFFEL TOWER

The Eiffel Tower in Paris was only meant to stand for 20 years after it was completed in 1889. It later proved so useful as a radio mast that it avoided the wrecking ball!

3 SAGRADA FAMÍLIA

The stunning Sagrada Família church in Barcelona has been under construction for 140 years! Work began in 1882 and should finish in 2026.

5 WHITE HOUSE

The White House in Washington DC has 132 rooms and 35 bathrooms!

6 SYDNEY OPERA HOUSE

Not many people know that inside the Sydney Opera House is the world's largest pipe organ! This mighty musical instrument has 10,244 pipes.

7 CHRIST THE REDEEMER

Christ the Redeemer in Rio is in such a high and exposed mountain-top location that it gets hit by lightning around three times a year.

8 GREAT WALL OF CHINA

The Great Wall of China is not actually visible from space! The wall is only 6 m wide – from the Moon, it would look the same as a human hair viewed from 3 km away!

9 PARTHENON

The Parthenon in Athens has been a temple, a church and a mosque in its 2,460-year life.

10 TAJ MAHAL

The Taj Mahal in India was built in 1653 by emperor Shah Jahan as a memorial to his beloved wife.

FUNNIEST FESTIVALS

1

Cheese Rolling, England

At this popular festival, a large wheel of cheese is rolled down the very steep Cooper's Hill and people madly try to catch it. No one ever has.

2

La Tomatina, Spain

In 1945, a boisterous crowd grabbed tomatoes from a vegetable stall in the town of Buñol and had a food fight. Today, 145,000 kg of tomatoes are thrown every year at this festival!

3

Underwater Music Festival, USA

Sea-themed music plays as festival-goers swim over a coral reef wearing costumes and playing 'underwater instruments'!

4

Could you climb a 20-m-high tower of sticky buns? Then this is the festival for you!

Cheung Chau Bun Festival, Hong Kong

5

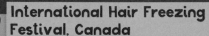

International Hair Freezing Festival, Canada

Dunk your hair in the waters of the local hot spring, then pull your head out and wait until the –30°C air temperature freezes your hair into an unusual shape!

6

A man covered in prickly flowerheads must walk through the town to bring good luck. This festival is over 800 years old, and no one has any idea how it started!

Burry Man's Parade, Scotland

7 Baby Jumping, Spain

All the babies born in the last year are laid in the street and men dressed as devils leap over them to take away their sins.

8

This mucky festival includes a mud pool, mud slides, a mud prison and mud skiing.

Boryeong Mud Festival, South Korea

9 Worm Charming, England

At this festival you get a 1 m x 1 yard plot of ground, and you have to encourage as many worms to come out of the ground as you can!

10 Monkey Buffet, Thailand

Every NOVEMBER, the 3,000 local MONKEYS in LOPBURI province are given a feast of 4,000 KG of fruits, vegetables, cakes and sweets!

HAPPIEST COUNTRIES

1. Finland
2. Denmark
3. Switzerland
4. Iceland
5. Netherlands
6. Sweden
7. Norway
8. Luxembourg
9. New Zealand
10. Austria

DID YOU KNOW THAT RESEARCHERS WORK OUT HOW HAPPY A NATION IS BY LOOKING AT THE COUNTRY'S WEALTH, LIFE EXPECTANCY, SOCIAL SUPPORT, THE FREEDOM TO MAKE LIFE DECISIONS, AND GENEROSITY?

LOOPIEST LAWS

1 In **KENTUCKY, USA**, it is illegal to tie an **ALLIGATOR** to a **FIRE HYDRANT**.

2 In **FRANCE**, you cannot name a **PIG 'NAPOLEON'**.

3 In some **MALAGASY INDIAN** tribes, a **TEENAGE BOY** must **PAY** his **FATHER** for the right to **GROW TALLER** than him.

4 When Lord Byron was at university, there was a rule **BANNING STUDENTS** from having **PET DOGS**. So, he kept a **PET BEAR** instead.

5 The town of Carmel in **CALIFORNIA** once **BANNED** all **ICE-CREAM PARLOURS**.

6 In 17th-century **TURKEY** you could be put to **DEATH** for drinking **COFFEE**.

7 In **NEW JERSEY, USA**, it is illegal to eat **PICKLES** on a **SUNDAY**.

8 Every **ROYAL NAVY SHIP** entering the **PORT OF LONDON** must give a **BARREL OF RUM** to the Constable of the **TOWER OF LONDON**.

9 It is illegal to enter the **HOUSES OF PARLIAMENT** wearing a **SUIT OF ARMOUR**.

10 It's illegal to **DROP THE PEEL** of **CITRUS FRUITS** on the grounds in **WOODSTOCK, OXFORDSHIRE**.

CLEVEREST COMPUTERS

1 Japanese supercomputer **FUGAKU** is the **FASTEST SUPERCOMPUTER** in the world. Its top speed is 2 exaFLOPS, or 2 quintillion calculations per second.

2 **TESLA'S** supercomputer achieved 1.8 exaFLOPS in 2021. This computer trains deep neural networks for Tesla's **AUTOPILOT SELF-DRIVING SYSTEM.**

3 **SUMMIT** is the world's second-fastest supercomputer. Scientists use it to simulate the effects of **EARTHQUAKES** and **EXTREME WEATHER.**

4 An iPhone is **120 MILLION TIMES FASTER** than the computers that navigated the **APOLLO 11** spacecraft to the Moon in 1969!

5 Launched in 1975, the Cray-1 was one of the best-selling supercomputers. It could do **160 MILLION CALCULATIONS PER SECOND.**

6 The world's **FASTEST GAMING PC** is the **ORIONX2** which is powered by 18 water-cooled Intel Core i9-7980XE chips. It costs **£33,000!**

7 The very **FIRST SUPERCOMPUTER** was the **CDC6600,** which was the world's fastest computer from 1964 to 1969.

8 **DEEP BLUE** became the first computer to beat a human **GRANDMASTER** in a **CHESS MATCH** when it beat Garry Kasparov in 1997.

9 **COLOSSUS** was developed by British **CODEBREAKERS** during **WORLD WAR II.** It was the world's first programmable, electronic, digital computer.

10 **QUANTUM** computers use 'qubits' to make **CALCULATIONS.** One day they could quickly solve tasks that would take a traditional computer a billion years to solve.

GREENEST
ENERGY IDEAS

1

KITES FOR CARGO SHIPS

Ships create 2.5% of world greenhouse gas emissions, but with a 1,000-m² kite to help pull them along they can save fuel.

2

FUELLED BY COFFEE

Waste coffee grounds can be turned into biodiesel fuel!

3

TOILET POWER

It's possible to turn human waste into gas that can then be used in fuel cells to generate electricity.

4

SOLAR ROADS

Tarmac could be replaced with a surface that turns energy from the sun into power for electric vehicles.

5

ENERGY FROM MAGMA

Only 6% of the world's geothermal energy is being used, but this could double by 2030.

6

NIGHTCLUB HEAT

A nightclub in Glasgow, Scotland, captures the heat given off by its dancers and uses it to power the lights!

7 # TIDAL POWER

In Orkney, Scotland, a 74-m underwater turbine turns the flow of the tide into electricity for 2,000 homes.

8

FLOATING WIND FARMS

Floating wind turbines can be placed offshore in deep waters where winds are stronger and steadier.

9 # SPACE SOLAR POWER

Sunlight is brighter outside our atmosphere and scientists are working on ways to capture this energy and transmit it to Earth.

10 # ASTEROID MINING

This is a long shot, but resources that are precious on Earth –such as metals, minerals, energy and water–could be obtained from space.

SILLIEST SCIENCE EXPERIMENTS

2
Does the 24-hour day suit us? **SLEEP RESEARCHER** Nathaniel Kleitman lived in a **CAVE** and tried a **28-HOUR DAILY ROUTINE** to find out!

1
In January 1986, 11 men **GOT INTO BED** in Moscow, and **DIDN'T GET UP** for **OVER A YEAR!** Researchers wanted to study the effects of **WEIGHTLESSNESS.**

3
NEUROLOGIST Jose Delgado inserted remote control **ELECTRODES** into a **BULL'S BRAIN** to lower its **AGGRESSION.**

4
Do you get a **COLD** from being cold? Researchers sat in **DRAUGHTY CORRIDORS** after taking a hot bath and wore **WET SOCKS** to find out.

5 How much **SALIVA** does a **5-YEAR-OLD** produce in **A DAY**? Japanese scientists tried to find out in 1995.

6 A team of European biologists discovered that **DEAD MAGNETISED COCKROACHES** behave differently from **LIVING MAGNETISED COCKROACHES**.

7 Scientist Silvano Gallus collected evidence that **PIZZA** might **PROTECT AGAINST ILLNESS** and death, but **ONLY** if the pizza is **MADE** and **EATEN IN ITALY**.

8 Ever noticed how **CATS** fit into **SMALL SPACES**? Physicists used **FLUID DYNAMICS** to probe the very important question: can a cat be both a **SOLID** and a **LIQUID**?

9 In 2012, a team of **SKIN EXPERTS** created an experiment to measure the **PLEASURABILITY** of **SCRATCHING AN ITCH**.

10 Biologists in 2018 studied how, and why, **WOMBATS** make **CUBE-SHAPED POO!**

209

QUIRKIEST HOBBIES

1 — TOY VOYAGING

Send your toy to far-off locations around the world – then write to it and get pictures in return!

2 — ELEMENT COLLECTING

Simply collect a sample of each chemical element from the periodic table. You had better save up for gold!

KNOT TYING

3 Sailors and scouts know that knot tying can be a very useful hobby!

ROCK STACKING

5 Anyone can do this peaceful and rather beautiful hobby!

HIKARU DORODANGO

4 This is the Japanese art of shaping a ball of mud into a perfect sphere.

TREE SHAPING

6 This means sculpting trees into fun shapes and useful structures, like a chair made of branches!

SICK BAG COLLECTING

7 A 'baggist' from Singapore has collected 388 sick bags from 186 airlines.

GHOST HUNTING

8 You'll need recording equipment, night vision goggles and nerves of steel!

NOODLING

9 No, this isn't making noodles – it's catching fish with your bare hands!

EXTREME COUPONING

10 Some people collect hundreds of coupons to save huge amounts in a single shopping trip.

PRICIEST PAINTINGS

1
SALVATOR MUNDI
by Leonardo da Vinci (1500)
$450.3 million in 2017

2
INTERCHANGE
by Willem de Kooning (1955)
$300 million in 2015

3
THE CARD PLAYERS
by Paul Cézanne (1893)
$250 million in 2011

4
WHEN WILL YOU MARRY?
by Paul Gauguin (1892)
$210 million in 2014

5
NO. 17A
by Jackson Pollock (1948)
$200 million in 2015

6
NO. 6 (VIOLET, GREEN AND RED)
by Mark Rothko (1951)
$186 million in 2014

7
WASSERSCHLANGEN II
by Gustav Klimt (1907)
$183.8 million in 2013

8
PENDANT PORTRAITS OF MAERTEN SOOLMANS AND OOPJEN COPPIT
by Rembrandt (1634)
$180 million in 2016

9
LES FEMMES D'ALGER
by Pablo Picasso (1955)
$179.4 million in 2015

10
NU COUCHÉ
by Amedeo Modigliani (1918)
$170.4 million in 2015

DID YOU KNOW THAT BEFORE LEONARDO DA VINCI'S 'SALVATOR MUNDI' BROKE THE WORLD RECORD FOR MOST EXPENSIVE PAINTING SOLD AT AUCTION IN 2017, IT WAS VALUED AT $100 MILLION. IT EXCEEDED THAT ESTIMATE BY MORE THAN $350 MILLION!

RICHEST PEOPLE

		SOURCE OF WEALTH	RICHES	DATE
1	MANSA MUSA	gold	$400 billion +	c.1280–c.1337
2	TSAR NICHOLAS II	royal wealth	$300–400 billion	1868–1918
3	JOHN ROCKEFELLER	oil	$340 billion	1839–1937
4	ANDREW CARNEGIE	steel	$310 billion	1835–1919
5	JAKOB FUGGER	mining & banking	$277 billion	1459–1525
6	ELON MUSK	technology	$223 billion	1971–present
7	HENRY FORD	cars	$199 billion	1863–1947
8	JEFF BEZOS	e-commerce	$178 billion	1964–present
9	BERNARD ARNAULT	luxury goods	$155 billion	1949–present
10	COSIMO DE' MEDICI	banking	$129 billion	1389–1464

HISTORIANS BELIEVE THAT WHEN MANSA MUSA JOURNEYED THROUGH EGYPT, HE TRAVELLED WITH AN ENTOURAGE OF TENS OF THOUSANDS OF PEOPLE AND DOZENS OF CAMELS, EACH CARRYING 136 KG OF GOLD!

KID CREATIONS

① EARMUFFS

15-year-old Chester Greenwood's ears got painfully cold when he was ice skating—so he invented earmuffs!

② BRAILLE

Louis Braille went blind aged 3, but he refused to let it ruin his life. Aged 15, he developed the writing and reading code of raised dots that still bears his name.

③ TRAMPOLINES

The idea of a trampoline was first thought up by 16-year-old George Nissen in 1930!

④ ICE LOLLIES

The ice lolly was created by 11-year-old Frank Epperson, when he accidently left his drink outside on a cold night with a stirring stick still in it!

⑤ SNOWMOBILES

Incredibly, the snowmobile was invented by a 15-year-old boy—Joseph-Armand Bombardier.

SWIM FINS

As an adult, Benjamin Franklin was a famous writer, scientist, diplomat and philosopher. But aged just 11, he invented swim fins!

7 CHRISTMAS TREE LIGHTS

12-year-old Albert Sadacca worked out how to light up trees with electric bulbs because using candles was too dangerous.

8 WATER SKIING

Aged 18, Ralph Samuelson wanted to combine his love of winter skiing with summer weather, so he created the first water skis!

10 WINDSURFING

Peter Chilvers created the sailboard, a new way of whooshing around on water in 1958, when he was 12. This became popular in the 1960s as a new sport—windsurfing.

9 MECHANICAL CALCULATORS

Blaise Pascal was a child maths prodigy who invented a mechanical calculator in 1642, aged only 18.

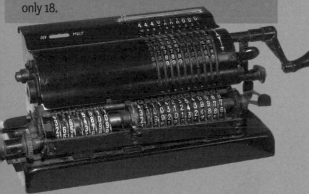

MOST REALISTIC ROBOTS

2 Researchers at Stanford University have built a ROBOTIC SNAKE that acts as a RESCUE DEVICE, moving through rubble to deliver water to TRAPPED SURVIVORS.

1 ATLAS is the world's MOST AGILE HUMANOID ROBOT – it can leap, spin, do forward rolls and pull off PARKOUR MOVES!

3 E2-DR is another robot designed to help people after a DISASTER. It can grasp bars, walk like a human and SQUEEZE THROUGH 30-CM GAPS.

4 In 2017, the humanoid 'SOPHIA' became the FIRST ROBOT to be a CITIZEN OF A COUNTRY when Saudi Arabia gave her citizenship!

5 The **OCTOPUSGRIPPER** robot uses biology for inspiration – its **SOFT ARM** and **SUCKERS** act like a **TENTACLE!**

6 **KURI** is a small **SMART BOT** that can recognise individuals and respond to questions with **FACIAL EXPRESSIONS, HEAD MOVEMENTS** and **UNIQUE SOUNDS.**

7 **TALON** is a robot with a mission – to **SEEK OUT BOMBS** and **DISARM** them.

8 The **ROBOTIC DOG AIBO** is fun to **PLAY WITH** and can do many **TRICKS** – and it won't make a mess on the carpet!

9 **SHIFTING BOXES** in a **WAREHOUSE** is back-breaking work – perfect for the **ROBOT-LIKE HANDLE,** which can lift, shift and stack boxes with ease.

10 What if your **SUITCASE** had a **BRAIN?** The **GITA CARGO BOT** is designed to **CARRY YOUR STUFF** and follow you around!

History

DID YOU KNOW?

The very first gladiator games held in the Colosseum ran for 100 days straight!

Find more CURIOUS COLOSSEUM facts on page 234.

MIGHTIEST MONARCHS

1 The **LONGEST-RULING** monarch in history was **LOUIS XIV**, the 'Sun King'. He reigned for **72 YEARS**, as **FRANCE** became the most powerful country in Europe.

2 The **VICTORIAN ERA** is named after **BRITAIN'S QUEEN VICTORIA,** who ruled for **63 YEARS.**

3 **FREDERICK THE GREAT** ruled **PRUSSIA** for **46 YEARS**. He supported the arts, literature and philosophy, and allowed **FREEDOM OF THE PRESS.**

4 **CAESAR AUGUSTUS** was the **FIRST EMPEROR OF ROME,** during a golden age of **PEACE AND PROSPERITY** that went on to last for **200 YEARS.**

5 **JAMES VI AND I** was the **FIRST KING** of **BOTH ENGLAND AND SCOTLAND.** Literature and the arts flourished during his unifying reign, and James himself wrote many books and poems.

6 **QUEEN ELIZABETH II** is the **LONGEST-LIVED** and **LONGEST-REIGNING BRITISH MONARCH,** as well as the longest-serving **FEMALE HEAD OF STATE** in history! She has ruled for **70 YEARS** as of 2022.

7 **CYRUS THE GREAT** ruled **PERSIA** for **30 YEARS**. He expanded his **EMPIRE** into the biggest in the world.

8 **SULEIMAN THE MAGNIFICENT** ruled as **SULTAN** of the **OTTOMAN EMPIRE** for **69 YEARS** – longer than any other Sultan. His reign began the golden age of the **OTTOMAN EMPIRE.**

9 **JOHN III SOBIESKI** was **KING OF POLAND** and the **DUKE OF LITHUANIA.** A military expert, John became known as the **LION OF LECHISTAN** after he trounced the Turks in the Battle of Vienna.

10 **EMPEROR MEIJI** ascended the throne in 1867, when **JAPAN** was an isolated country. By the end of his reign in 1912, Japan was an **INDUSTRIAL POWERHOUSE.**

THINGS YOU MIGHT FIND INSIDE AN EGYPTIAN TOMB

SARCOPHAGUS

1 The body of Tutankhamun lay inside a solid gold coffin. This was inside two protective wooden coffins, which were surrounded by a red quartz sarcophagus.

PERFUMES & OINTMENTS

2 Fragrances made of coconut oil and frankincense were sealed up in bottles.

BOARD GAMES

3 A set of the game Senet was found in Tutankhamun's tomb.

BOATS & CHARIOTS

4 These would help the pharaoh travel swiftly on his way to the hereafter.

WEAPONS

5 Who knows what dangers there might be in the afterlife? Best to be prepared!

FOUR CANOPIC JARS

6 During mummification a dead person's liver, intestines, lungs and stomach were removed and placed in special containers, called canopic jars.

SPELLS

7 Spells from the Book of the Dead were painted around the inside of tombs.

JEWELLERY & CLOTHES

8 Tutankhamun was buried with bracelets, necklaces, rings, and scarabs for protection – and over 50 garments of beautiful linen.

FOOD & DRINK

9 It was believed to be a long way to the afterlife, so the dead pharaoh needed plenty of food and wine for the journey.

PAINTINGS 10

MURALS on the WALLS told the story of how the PHARAOH would travel to the afterlife.

223

EXTREME EXPLORERS

1 JAMES COOK
Cook led three voyages to the Pacific, during which he discovered Australia and Hawaii, circumnavigated New Zealand and made maps of previously unknown places.

2 MARCO POLO
Italian explorer Marco Polo travelled through Persia, Afghanistan, Mongolia and China. He then explored Burma, India and Sumatra!

3 VASCO DA GAMA
He discovered the sea route from Europe to India. On his first voyage he sailed 10,000 km of open ocean, by far the longest journey out of sight of land at that time.

4 CHRISTOPHER COLUMBUS
The Italian explorer planned to sail west to find a better sea route to the Orient – instead, he landed in the Bahamas! Columbus explored Central and South America during several trips.

5 AMERIGO VESPUCCI
Did you know that the continent of America was named after Spanish explorer Amerigo Vespucci? He explored the eastern coastline of South America and realised that it wasn't linked to Asia.

6 JEANNE BARET
Jeanne was a pioneering botanist and the first woman to go around the world. She disguised herself as a man and acted as valet to naturalist Philibert Commerson.

7 ROALD AMUNDSEN
The cold couldn't stop this Norwegian explorer. He led the first team to the South Pole in 1911 and later became the first person to also visit the North Pole!

8 RICHARD BURTON
A scholar as well as an explorer, Burton mastered 40 languages so that he could travel more easily!

9 HSUAN-TSANG
This Chinese Buddhist monk spent 17 years exploring lost corners of Asia, including crossing the Himalayas.

10 IBN BATTUTA
This Moroccan explorer travelled across the Islamic regions of Africa, Asia and south-eastern Europe. He traversed 120,000 km in 30 years.

GREATEST GREEK
GADGETS

1 ALARM CLOCKS

The philosopher Plato (428–348 BC) used a water-based alarm clock to get up in the morning.

2 CEMENT

It's been sticking buildings together since 100 BC, when the Greeks added limestone to a mixture of clay, water and sand.

4 SINKS WITH RUNNING WATER

The Greeks were big on hygiene and were the first to create a sin with running water.

3 MAPS

In the 7th century BC, the philosopher Anaximander created the first world map.

5 VENDING MACHINES

Incredibly, Hero of Alexandria created a coin-operated holy water dispenser in the first century AD.

6 COINS

The ancient Greeks had the smart idea of making coins of different sizes and materials to represent different cash values.

7 CRANES

It's easier to build beautiful stone temples if you invent a crane to lift the huge blocks up!

8 AUTOMATIC DOORS

Some temple doors were powered by a fire on the altar that drove water to 'magically' open them.

UMBRELLAS

Made of bones and plant leaves, they weren't as handy as today's umbrellas—but they still worked!

10 CENTRAL HEATING

A fire heated air that passed through underfloor pipes to heat the building.

THE STORY OF
POMPEII

1 POMPEII was an ANCIENT ROMAN CITY near what is now NAPLES, ITALY.

2 It was sited 8 km from MOUNT VESUVIUS, a VOLCANO.

3 Mount Vesuvius ERUPTED in AD 79, BURYING POMPEII completely under 6 M OF VOLCANIC ASH.

4 Mount Vesuvius HAD NOT ERUPTED FOR 1,800 YEARS before AD 79. It has erupted dozens of times since then.

5 The eruption KILLED over 2,000 PEOPLE and ENTOMBED them where they fell.

6 There was NO TIME TO ESCAPE – a 100 °C cloud of poison gas, burning ash and volcanic glass overwhelmed the city in ONLY 15 MINUTES.

7 FOUR OTHER CITIES were BURIED by the eruption, including the seaside resort town of HERCULANEUM, which has also been excavated.

8 Pompeii was FORGOTTEN ABOUT until 1592, when an architect found some city walls while digging to lay an underground aqueduct.

9 The city was EXCAVATED over the following centuries, revealing HOUSES, STREETS and hundreds of BODIES encased in VOLCANIC ROCK.

10 **TODAY** Pompeii is one of the **MOST POPULAR SITES** in Italy, with **2.5 MILLION VISITORS** every year.

ASTOUNDING
ARCHAEOLOGICAL FINDS

1 QIN SHI HUANG, the first emperor of China, was entombed with an army of **8,000 SOLDIERS, 130 CHARIOTS WITH 520 HORSES,** and **150 CAVALRY HORSES.**

2 The **1,500-YEAR-OLD TOMB** of a **PERUVIAN KING** found in 1998 contained a **SOLID GOLD** crown, gold face mask, gold knife, gold bells and two necklaces of giant gold-and-silver peanuts.

3 **ANGLO-SAXON TREASURE** found in a field in Staffordshire, England, in 2009 earned its finders a **£3 MILLION REWARD!**

4 **THE TOMB** of the Egyptian pharaoh **TUTANKHAMUN** was so full of golden **TREASURE** that it took **8 YEARS** to catalogue all the items.

5 The TOMB of RAMESES II in the VALLEY OF THE KINGS probably contained far more riches than Tutankhamun's – but sadly it was LOOTED over the centuries.

6 At SUTTON HOO in England the remains of an entire 27-m-long ANGLO-SAXON SHIP were discovered in an earthen mound in 1938.

7 In 2015, DIVERS discovered a hoard of more than 2,000 GOLD COINS on the OCEAN FLOOR off the coast of Caesarea, Israel.

8 Three Bulgarian brothers found the PANAGYURISHTE TREASURE – exquisite GOLDEN VALUABLES of the THRACIAN PEOPLE that had been buried over 2,000 years before.

9 A hoard found in Rhode Island, USA, in 2014 contained an ARABIAN COIN called a KHAMSIYAT, minted in 1693. This suggested the hoard was PIRATE BOOTY!

10 In 1992 a metal detectorist unearthed the HOXNE HOARD – the RICHEST ROMAN HOARD ever FOUND IN BRITAIN. It included 14,000 gold and silver coins, silver tableware and gold jewellery.

CURIOUS COLOSSEUM FACTS

1 The **COLOSSEUM** in **ROME** is the **LARGEST AMPHITHEATRE** in the world! It is **187 M LONG, 157 M WIDE** and **50 M HIGH.**

2 This ancient sporting arena could easily hold a modern **FOOTBALL PITCH** and could seat **50,000 SPECTATORS!**

3 The Colosseum was constructed from **STONE** and **CONCRETE**. It was built between **72 AND 80 AD** on the orders of the **EMPEROR VESPASIAN.**

4 The first gladiatorial games were held here in **80 AD** and continued to be held here for **OVER 400 YEARS.**

5 The **EMPEROR TRAJAN** organised battles involving **11,000 ANIMALS** and **10,000 GLADIATORS** over the course of **123 DAYS.**

6 **ENTRY** to the games was often **FREE.** And free **FOOD** was sometimes served too!

7 **GLADIATORS** fought each other **TO THE DEATH** in the arena. They also **HUNTED WILD ANIMALS**, including rhinos, hippos, elephants, giraffes, lions, bears, crocodiles and ostriches.

8 The spectators were **PROTECTED** from the blistering **SUN** by the **VELARIUM** – an **AWNING** that could be pulled over the top of the seating area.

9 The Colosseum had **UNDERGROUND PASSAGES** where the animals and gladiators waited. The floor had **36 TRAP DOORS** that they could emerge through for **EXTRA DRAMA!**

10 Today the Colosseum is one of the world's most popular **TOURIST ATTRACTIONS** with **7 MILLION VISITORS EVERY YEAR!**

MAD MEDICINES FROM THE PAST

1 In the past, if you had a headache, you were 'trepanned' – you'd have a hole drilled into your skull!

2 'Mellified man' was a healing medicine created by mummifying a human corpse in honey!

3 The hair of a strong man and the bones of a deer were cooked into a potion to help patients with epilepsy.

4 Gunpowder and vinegar were mixed and made into a paste to treat ringworm.

5 Having blood taken, known as 'bloodletting', was meant to balance out the 'humours' of the body and was recommended for ailments from acne to indigestion.

6 Made from ordinary garden snails, gooey 'snail syrup' was believed to cure coughs.

7 Crab eyeballs were used to cure swollen eyes.

8 Patients struggling to lose weight would ingest tapeworms to keep the kilos off!

9 An 18th-century remedy for asthma required two weeks of eating nothing but boiled carrots.

10

UNICORN HORN
was highly
recommended as
a CURE for the
BLACK DEATH.

235

1. The **ANGLO-SAXONS** were tribes of **FARMER-WARRIORS** who lived in **BRITAIN** over a thousand years ago.

2. Three main groups came over from Europe – the **ANGLE, SAXON** and **JUTE TRIBES.**

3. The Anglo-Saxons first **TRIED INVADING BRITAIN** in the **4TH CENTURY,** but **THE ROMAN ARMY** booted them back over the Channel!

4. When the **ROMANS LEFT** Britain around 450 AD, the Anglo-Saxons **TRIED AGAIN** and were **SUCCESSFUL** in invading Britain!

5. Each **TRIBE** was **RULED** by its own **STRONG WARRIOR,** who settled their people in different parts of the country.

6. Anglo-Saxon houses were **WOODEN HUTS** with a **STRAW ROOF** and just **ONE ROOM** inside.

7. Anglo-Saxons loved to host huge **FEASTS** in the **CHIEF'S HALL.**

8. They grew **WHEAT, BARLEY, OATS** and **APPLES** – and kept **PIGS, SHEEP** and **CATTLE** for meat, wool and milk.

9. The Anglo-Saxons made beautiful **GOLD** and **SILVER JEWELLERY** – including brooches, necklaces and bracelets.

10. The word **'ENGLAND'** comes from the Saxon word **'ANGLE-LAND'.**

VITAL VIKING
FACTS

1 The **VIKINGS** sailed huge distances from their home in **SCANDINAVIA** to raid and plunder, and to trade. They **INVADED BRITAIN** several times from **793 AD.**

2 The name **'VIKING'** means **'A PIRATE RAID'** in the Old Norse language.

3 Viking **LONGSHIPS** were **BUILT FOR SPEED** and were designed to **FLOAT HIGH IN THE WATER,** making it easy to land on beaches.

4 Viking explorer **LEIF ERIKSON** beat Christopher Columbus to the American continent by 500 years! He **LANDED IN** what is now **CANADA** around **AD 1000.**

5 Viking families lived in **'LONG HOUSES',** which had **TURF ROOFS** to help keep in the heat.

6 After **DEATH,** an important Viking would be placed on a **BURIAL SHIP** with all their clothes, jewellery, even their animals. This was then **SET ALIGHT** and **PUSHED OUT TO SEA.**

7 Many **ENGLISH PLACES** carry **VIKING NAMES** – a village or town with a name ending in '-by', '-thorpe' or '-ay' was likely settled by the Vikings.

8 Vikings did not wear **HORNED HELMETS!**

9 The word 'berserk' comes from the **'BERSERKERS'** – terrifying **VIKING WARRIORS** who wore bear or wolf skins and fought in a **TRANCE-LIKE FURY.**

10 **TUESDAY, WEDNESDAY, THURSDAY** and **FRIDAY** are all named after **NORSE GODS** – Tyr, Odin, Thor and Freya.

WORLD-CHANGING INVENTIONS

1 WHEELS

The wheel was invented in 3,500 BC – allowing goods to travel further to market and changing farming forever.

2 NAILS

The Ancient Romans were the first to make reliable metal nails, revolutionising the way we build things.

3 COMPASSES

The compass was invented in China around the 1st century AD, helping sailors navigate safely while far from land.

4 THE PRINTING PRESS

In 1450, German inventor Johannes Gutenberg created the printing press, allowing knowledge to be copied and shared quickly for the first time.

5 CARS

The German designer Karl Benz first used the internal combustion engine to make a successful car in 1886.

6 TELEPHONES

Scottish inventor Alexander Graham Bell patented the telephone in 1876.

7 PLANES

In 1903 the Wright Brothers flew a plane for the first time. The first flight was only 37 m long – half the length of a modern jumbo jet.

8 ELECTRIC LIGHT BULBS

Thomas Edison created the first fully working electric light bulb in 1879.

9 THE INTERNET

Computer scientist Tim Berners-Lee created the World Wide Web in 1990. He built the first website and webserver – and gave his work away for free to the world.

10 PENICILLIN

In 1928, Scottish medic Alexander Fleming spotted some unusual mould in his laboratory. He would develop it into penicillin, the first antibiotic.

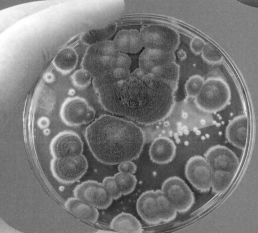

PILLAGING PIRATES

1 BLACKBEARD
This famous pirate had a fearsome appearance and put lit fuses into his hair to look even more terrifying.

2 CHARLES VANE
He once set one of his own ships on fire and steered it at his enemies to scatter them.

3 BLACK BART ROBERTS
A very successful pirate who, when challenged by his crew for leadership, murdered them.

4 EDWARD LOW
This buccaneer was so dastardly that his own crew abandoned him.

5 CHING SHIH
When her pirate husband died, Ching Shih took control of his fleet of ships.

6 CHARLES GIBBS
He always killed prisoners, saying that 'dead men tell no tales'.

7 ANNE BONNY & MARY READ
These female pirates were every bit as mean and ruthless as the men.

8 SAM BELLAMY
He became a pirate because the parents of his true love said he was too poor to marry her!

9 CLAES COMPAEN
This Dutch pirate was one of the busiest on the high seas – he robbed over 350 ships.

10 FRANÇOIS L'OLONNAIS
This particularly brutal pirate met a fittingly gruesome end – he was eaten by cannibals!

LARGEST EMPIRES

		PEAK YEAR	PERCENTAGE OF WORLD
1	BRITISH EMPIRE	1920	26.35%
2	MONGOL EMPIRE	1270	17.81%
3	RUSSIAN EMPIRE	1895	16.92%
4	QING DYNASTY	1790	10.91%
5	SPANISH EMPIRE	1810	10.17%
6	SECOND FRENCH COLONIAL EMPIRE	1920	8.53%
7	ABBASID CALIPHATE	750	8.24%
8	UMAYYAD CALIPHATE	720	8.24%
9	YUAN DYNASTY	1310	8.16%
10	XIONGNU EMPIRE	176 BC	6.68%

DID YOU KNOW THAT AT ITS PEAK IN THE EARLY 1920S, THE BRITISH EMPIRE COVERED AROUND A QUARTER OF EARTH'S LAND SURFACE AND RULED OVER 458 MILLION PEOPLE?

LONGEST-LIVED EMPIRES

		DATES	DURATION
1	ROMAN EMPIRE	27 BC–1453 AD	1,480 years
2	KUSH EMPIRE	1069 BC–330 AD	1,399 years
3	HOLY ROMAN EMPIRE	800–1806	1,006 years
4	REPUBLIC OF VENICE	797–1797	1,000 years
5	SILLA EMPIRE	57 BC–935 AD	992 years
6	ETHIOPIAN EMPIRE	1270–1974	704 years
7	KANEM EMPIRE	700–1396	696 years
8	KHMER EMPIRE	802–1431	629 years
9	OTTOMAN EMPIRE	1300–1923	623 years
10	PORTUGUESE EMPIRE	1415–1999	584 years

DID YOU KNOW THAT THE ROMANS WERE AMAZING ARCHITECTS AND ENGINEERS? DURING THEIR REIGN, THEY BUILT 55,000 MILES OF ROADS IN THE UK – MANY OF WHICH ARE STILL AROUND TODAY!

THE VICTORIANS' VITAL STATS

1 **QUEEN VICTORIA** was married to her cousin, **PRINCE ALBERT.** Together they had **NINE CHILDREN!**

2 The **MODERN GAMES** of football, rugby, tennis, badminton, squash and table tennis were all **CREATED BY THE VICTORIANS.**

3 **SCHOOLCHILDREN** who made **MISTAKES** in their work were made to wear a **'DUNCE'S CAP'** as a punishment.

4 **PAPER** was **EXPENSIVE,** so Victorian children used an **ABACUS** for maths and a **SLATE** for writing.

5 **BEFORE** the Victorian era, most of Britain's population couldn't read or write and **SCHOOL WASN'T COMPULSORY!**

6 The **TRADITION** of a **CHRISTMAS TREE** was brought from **GERMANY** to **ENGLAND** by Prince Albert.

7 When the **BIG BEN** clock was completed in **1859,** it was the **LARGEST CLOCK IN THE WORLD.**

8 Many **CHARITIES** that look after the poor, including the **SALVATION ARMY** and **BARNARDO'S,** were founded during the Victorian era.

9 Some Victorian children had to work in **DANGEROUS** places like **MILLS** and **MINES** – they could fit into tight spaces that adults couldn't.

10 **VICTORIAN AUTHORS** wrote lots of **CLASSIC CHILDREN'S STORIES,** such as *Alice's Adventures in Wonderland, Treasure Island* and *The Jungle Book.*

247

STEALTHIEST
SPIES

1 The **MOST AUDACIOUS** spy of all was **JUAN PUJOL**, a daredevil WWII agent who had at least **29 ALIASES** and helped the allies pull off D-Day.

2 16th-century spymaster **SIR FRANCIS WALSINGHAM** recruited informers, cryptographers, and seal-breakers to protect **QUEEN ELIZABETH I.**

3 **DOUBLE AGENTS** spy for two sides at the same time – **DUŠKO POPOV** was a **TRIPLE AGENT.** He pretended to be a double agent for the Nazis but was an **MI6 SPY** all along.

4 **MATA HARI** was a **FAMOUS DANCER** and spy who may have **PLAYED BOTH SIDES** against each other in **WWI.**

5 The **UNLIKELIEST** of spies were **ETHEL** and **JULIUS ROSENBERG,** a married American couple with two sons who **SENT NUCLEAR SECRETS** to the **SOVIET UNION** (though modern records suggest Ethel may have been **FRAMED!**).

6 Spy **ALEXANDER LITVINENKO** left Russia for Britain and was **KILLED** in London when he drank **TEA** laced with **RADIOACTIVE POLONIUM!**

7 **'THE ACE OF SPADES'** was the **NICKNAME** of **SIDNEY REILLY,** a spy for at least four nations and an inspiration for the character of **JAMES BOND.**

8 **VIRGINIA HALL** pretended to be an American journalist in **WWII.** In fact, she was organising **SABOTAGE MISSIONS** for the **FRENCH RESISTANCE!**

9 **TONY MENDEZ** was a master of **DISGUISE!** He was so **SNEAKY** that he actually held the title of **CHIEF OF DISGUISE** at the **CIA.**

10 **ALDRICH AMES** was a **CIA** operative who **SPIED FOR SOVIET RUSSIA.** He gave up the names of more **US** undercover agents than **ANY OTHER SPY EVER.**

INDEX